JINKS

JINKS

By

Monk Rose

ISBN 1-58721-144-0

1stBooks – Rev. 3/30/00

About the Book

A hard-luck youth triumphs over the calamities he has brought to those who sheltered him.

Jinks is a story told in the haunting blue-collar voice of an amiable innocent. Orphaned and itinerant, he seeks a place of safety among society's outcasts in the cities and forests of his nation, seeming always to walk the line between crisis and deliverance.

After an event in which he swings the axe in a tragic accident, he flees from the snowy logging camps of the northwest to the somnolence of the Everglades. Now small calamities trail him: machines break down, healthy people fall ill, good fortune fails, all best laid plans are scrambled.

One such catastrophe draws him into the reach of a powerful woman and her accomplice who entangle him in a murderous scheme, but the misfortune he brings everywhere with him now punishes these plotters. Unexpectedly, the events that free him also lead to the salvation of an entire town that nurtured him in darker days.

Gently comic and wise, JINKS is a joyous tale of one man's dogged spirit, and of moral justice that celebrates the bright promise of human goodwill.

S.S.O. HQ. TELETYPE TEL:1-644-288-3469   5:16 No.003   P.01

FOR LAW ENFORCEMENT USE ONLY

ROGER McMICHAELS

SNOHOMISH COUNTY SHERIFF'S OFFICE

4627 EDGECOMB TERRACE   P.O.BOX 46401

EVERETT, WASHINGTON

TO:LEE COUNTY SHERIFF'S OFFICE

87 POINCIANA PLACE

FORT MYERS,FL

RE YOUR INQUIRY DATED OCT 22, NO DEATH CERTIFICATE CONFIRMED
ISSUED FRANZ KORSAKOW ENTIRE NETWORK SCANNED 1960-PRESENT
NO RECORD FOUND ANTON KORSAKOW, ANDY KORSO, FRANK FARLEY, GREG
LOOMIS ENTIRE NETWORK SCANNED 1960-PRESENT. REGRET CANNOT BE MORE
HELP THESE INDIVIDUALS.

1

Andy Korso

Father, you can tell them now, I am <u>not</u> Harry Baranski. The alligators got him same as his daddy Peter Paul ahead of him, though I would bet a sawbuck they both were stiff before they hit the swamps. Six years apart. Remember, the papers said it was Greg Loomis underwater in Harry Baranski's car? Not true, never true. I am Greg Loomis-- or to be straight about it, I am the one that was called Greg Loomis back then, one of the trick names I used when trouble showed up. Also I was never cut out for business like Harry Baranski.

Me, I'm a little man, although I didn't mean to be. A pastor once told me I am covered with emotional lint, but if I do good deeds, my soul may still go down in perpetchatuitary. Yes, that is the way he said it. The truth is, I am not good for much except use of an axe-- which might have started me in this mess. My daddy taught us the use of it-- my brother & me-- for he was a woodsman before he came over here from the old country. We never had much school except a few times for a week or so; it would have brought our folks to danger, but snuck out every morning to collect junk-- paper, rags, metals-- to sell to the junkman and bring back a few nickels & dimes no matter what city we lived in at the time. I am writing this to you, Father, so's you can tell all the people who knew me how I fooled them so long with a lie. I learnt trusting and how to be wise from everybody there in town, then left them all worse off when I went away. I am bad luck and could not pay back what I owed without the lie.

I was born at home and it was told to me that my mama had a hard time working me out of her which fixed it so she couldn't have anymore babies. Next, when I was still little and not walking yet, one day my daddy held me in his arms and bent down to light his cigar off a gas burner in the kitchen stove and a spark sailed up in his eye. He dropped me then and I bounced off the stove onto his foot and broke it.

"That one is a bad luck baby," my daddy said a neighbor told him and they all laughed, he said, and he laughed again when he told me about it. He could not walk for a week nor work for a month, so it is not funny and is another reason I am in this mess; being a bad luck baby.

Up till I was eight or nine, wherever I went there was accidents-- dishes dropping, pets getting squashed, valuable things lost. Once at the county fair-- the only time my daddy took us, my brother & me-- the hot air balloon lost all its hot air when a storm came up and crashed some trees where six passengers climbed out and yowled like monkeys in the branches. Lightning struck and boiled five of them. I ran all the way home before they could blame me. After I was nine, all I ever been in company of is grownups and never got the hang of children.

Those days, I was Andy Korso, not my real name, but the one I used back then when I got smart enough to make the changes after the immigration people caught my parents and deported them back overseas for sneaking in the USA. I think somehow that is my fault too, Father, though it is so long ago and I was so young I can't bring the whole thing of it to mind.

Always on the lookout, my mother hid us in the neighbors one day when the vans pulled in through the project, and the neighbors threw us out as soon as the immigration left. They said Sorry we can't help it, most of us snuck in like your folks, but I never blamed them for it being nine years old, old enough to be glad about half a loaf. That was in the 60's sometime, when the government was nuts about illegal aliens, especially overseas. A year or two later, word got back to us that our mother and father jumped overboard and drowned, leaving us orphans without parents and no record of birth, which also in a way is another reason for this mess.

Lately I been thinking my parents did not jump overboard and drown but that somebody gave them a shove, for I been finding that people will do anything to profit, though it is hard to imagine what profit could be made by killing them, poor, so poor they were.

Ralph-- that's my brother-- Ralph is two years older than me. Well, I should say <u>was</u> two years older, and this will get me back

2

to the axe story. We started our runaway by hiding out and hitching rides on anything moving west, two kids with cardboard suitcases wearing old clothes. I remember Pennsylvania was hard because it was a worn out state down on its luck and there didn't seem to be many rides. Ohio was better. We caught two freights in Ohio took us clear into Indiana. I was too young then to know about beautiful valleys and mountains, but Ralph loved them and pointed them out to me. Also the frost and the first flat rays of the sun, he said. He made sure we were clean, finding soap in gas station bathrooms and scrubbing himself with his shirt off and then soaping me up; but what I remember most is being hungry, and that got us into stealing. We learnt to hang around school buildings early in the morning before the milk & baked goods were delivered, and when they were, snatch a few cartons and cakes for the road. Once in Iowa a nice lady made sandwiches seeing us and our suitcases after we told her we had no folks. She told us a poem I never forgot:

Some folks say a heart's like a suit,
You just wear it.
Other folks say it ain't a heart
Till you share it.

We did not steal from her, but when you have to steal it is handy being a kid and being poor because pity is as high in people's hearts as laughter without nearly as many ways to let it loose. Pity moves them quicker than a big stick. Pity lets them forgive. "That's the good of people," I used to think way back then when I was little and hungry all the time, though I had a hard time with that idea till recently.

At last we made timber country and what happened to Ralph out there -- and me being the fault of it-- always stuck with me ever since. It is a bad memory, and I been thinking it is like you have ahold of something mean you don't really want to keep but must keep and you are left not knowing how to hold it without touching it anymore. Like how does a cop handcuff a one-armed crook?

We took new names and found chores in lumber camps where gang bosses didn't ask questions but only supposed that kids who hung around-- and there were plenty besides us-- must belong to one or another of the loggers or sawyers. Nobody ever not once asked about why the kids were not in school, and we worked the seasons in peace a couple years or so living in the camps or sometimes a room in a nearby town. Then in October the third year, Ralph & me got hired on as cleanup hands at Roberson's saw-mill near Smith's Ferry on the North Fork of the Payette River in Idaho. Mr. Roberson himself was there that day at the camp and took a liking to Ralph who he approved the taking care of me, his baby brother.

"You must be a kind boy," he told Ralph, "a very kind boy. I know the sacrifice, for I brung up two sisters & a little brother myself when we was dumped in these woods twenty years ago after the war when the Japs surrendered." Then he stopped, like his face hurt, like he already said too much in front of the men. "Your little brother is sure a runt," he said and mussed my hair. I wondered then if his folks got deported too. I didn't know there were so many other reasons for children to get dumped. Mr. Roberson was big and bald, with a bass drum voice and he wore suspenders with also a belt. He once said, "You live with a woman for forty years, and before you know it, she thinks she's one of the family." As it turned out, we never heard the rest of his story.

Part of our new job was getting to the logging site and cutting out new growth to make room so the work gangs could be trucked in, and we had our hands full with pine, birch, beech and oak. Then one day, with the ground frosted crusty like toast and the saws already whining and screaming, I took my two-pound doublebit and Ralph took his four-pounder and we made off for the clearing, a mile or so in before the men had their coffee. Dusty Broom-- his real name-- came along for he took a shine to us right away and said he would make it his business to see we stayed clear of trouble till we got the hang of things. He said poison weeds would get in our blood if we touched them and poison snakes likewise. And bear, he said; bear could snatch your hand off in a single bite or otherwise swat you so hard with claws your head would roll like a bowling ball. He told us that actually happened once on a dear old friend he could not right then recall the name of. Dusty had eyes blue and hard as the agates I remember little kids play with in the playground on those few times Ralph & me tried school. His hair was whiskery like pine needles, and he bragged he had never took a razor to his beard, full and dark and tangled like a horsehair mattress. He wore galluses and a belt like Mr. Roberson and also most of the other cutters wore too for the strain of the axe hits you hard in the shoulders and hips, and he sometimes talked French or put a French twist on regular words from the way he hung around with the Canadian loggers which he said had the lucky mark of good fortune in their spirit. I heard him myself once when an old woods tramp asked him for the loan of a quarter, he said, "Voyla toot mon avwar," and gave the poor man a dime, which he said meant Here is the last penny in my clutch. "All folks think about is money," he said.

It was Dusty let us in on his sons. One night he was boiling coffee for the three of us-- him and Ralph and me-- and a breeze came up stiff & hard enough to blaze the coals. "Nobody talks about the wind, but it's the wind what doubles the punch because they are winter born and come up without warnin'. I'm talkin' about avalanches. In winter the snow is dry like powder and the snowfields can only hold so much before they let fall. You are never ready for a winter avalanche. Them what come in the spring they are more regular because the sun heats things up and water collects below the snowbanks and loosens it from the ground and the fields slip down. I know about avalanches; I lost both my boys to one. It is why I don't do no cuttin' near the mountains no more."

Ralph was too polite to ask so I said, "You could help us with the story in case we get stuck out someplace next to a mountain."

Dusty didn't need the prod. He would of talked to the owls. "I didn't want my boys to be loggers for it is a hard life with danger all the way and no pot of gold at the end. You are lucky if you miss frostbite and don't starve snowed-in trapped in a line cabin ten miles from the motor pool. You are lucky if you count both hands and ten fingers after it is over. I told my sons all about it, but naturally that is what they done anyway. I made sure they learnt trades in school. Cornelius was a cabinet maker and Pushkin done rough framing for builders. So what's the first thing they do out of school? They go with the National Forest Service to be in the wild! Pushkin done the stringers and studwork for tower shacks and Cornelius done the interior finishing."

I didn't think of it till I was grown some and learnt more, but Dusty Broom's boys names-- Cornelius & Pushkin-- was absolut-ely meant to be called Corn Broom & Push Broom. Names are a joke parents play on babies and I am happy I learnt the trick of changing my own, though it has always been for safety and not beauty that I did it.

"<u>Le garde forestee-ay</u>," Dusty said. He pulled the coffeepot off the fire and whanged it on the side to loose up the grinds stuck to the insides and then wished it around for flavor. I saw he was expert in all woods things.

"The Rangers, my boys finally wanted to be Rangers. You know what Rangers got to do? They must know the forests of the world-- Africa, West Indies, North America, South America, New Zealand & Australia, Europe, Russia, India. They must know climates and rainfall and floods, and laws and grafting and foods and dyes and fiber, and game and planting and bugs and diseases. They must know <u>Petrified</u>, where trees a hunnert million years ago fell in the water and got buried in clay and the water took out the wood and put in the stone. But they do not learn about avalanches."

The coffee was boiled bitter but Dusty swallowed it and smacked his lips and clapped his knee. "Man, that's good!" he hollered. "Damn near as good as whiskey. And that reminds me of another thing-- will power. You know what will power is? It is when you are too drunk to crawl to your bottle. A-haw-caw!" he laughed like a crow.

"They do not learn about avalanches," Ralph said, to bump him back on the track.

Dusty sucked his beard a minute and shook his head. "Right. Yes, they do not learn about avalanches. I wanted my boys to be safe in the city. I was scared the forest'd lay its stain in they hearts. Well, they was in Washington one winter and here come a storm so sudden and big they got caught up in a tower shack they was finishing with no place to run. Sixty foot in the air, Cornelius and Pushkin and a Ranger name Dell, Franklin D. Dell, a college boy. Called Bosky for short by his friends. The tower was at the ankle of Mount Bonaparte, 7267 foot high, twenty mile east of the Okanogan River and 20 mile south of the Canada border. It was cold and the wind come in at 40, 45 knots at first. Boys, you ever been stuck at the ankle of a mountain in a blizzard?"

"No, no sir, Dusty," Ralph said. I could tell he was hungry for this story and would eat it up whole. Me, I begun to get scared.

"You can not ever forget it, the wind. Starts out a-moanin' like a hurt dog, then picks up force-- 50, 60 knot gusts and the snow already shut out all the light, blowin' at you till the sound is a woman's scream, you can't tell the difference. Ranger Franklin D. Dell lived to tell about it, and he says the ice blowed like fists on a face. He told me the tower begun to shake and rumble, and the shack up top where him and the boys was, it skewed. The temperature dropped 20 points in a half hour and everything a man could see and touch was covered, rapped and clutched in ice. So Ranger Dell, he told Cornelius and Pushkin to stay put and he would go for help. It took him 40 minutes to go down them steps-- 101 steps in ice near an inch thick."

Dusty Broom's hand was shaking with the coffee slopping over the sides of his cup. He ran his sleeve under his nose, and Ralph took the cup and patted him on the shoulder. Dusty breathed easier and Ralph went and poured him a fresh cup.

"Sorry boys, I miss my sons, is all." He sipped the coffee and smacked his lips again. "Second cup as good as the first," he said, setting it down and smiling a little at us. "Sirens and distress signals all up and down the Okanogan, the whole northeast shank of the state got it, even some down through Oregon. Cars, boats marooned, left where they was, without harbor, without garages. Buildings lost they roofs, a whole high school dropped its top floor and the school bus got blowed off a bridge

7

downriver, no survivors. I must think my boys was prayin' for the night to be over but when daylight broke it was only to see the northwest face of Mount Bonaparte above them, bigger and closer from what the blizzard brung in and added on. Ranger Dell told me all this because he spent the night on snowshoes and lost his way two miles from the tower bundled in the rugs he brung with him. He was just started on the way back to the tower when he seen what happened, how the wind stopped and the dead calm set in and the mountain begun to shift when powder snow slipped, puffs and squirts like you blow smoke from the side of your mouth whilst your lips is shut. And then the avalanche come. With noise that turn you to stone and a wind to take the hair off your chin. When it was over, the tower was down under 30 foot of snow and all the pines for a square mile around had they needles blowed off; not a single one left. Nor my boys." He made a big sigh. "Folks keep callin' this the in-between, this life, but sooner or later they find out it's the <u>it</u>."

Then he told us to come by him and warm up near the fire.

*

Next day, when we got to the clearing, Dusty marked off an alley eight foot by twenty which would bend down to the dirt road once we got it cut for the trucks to roll in. Then he smacked his hands together loud as wood clappers and begun shearing saplings right at ground level with one big swipe like there was nothing in the world but him and his axe and the next growth. Then Ralph and me jumped in, watching him, copying him, and soon started sweating like him when the sun showed and the bugs buzzed and the new day showed in the woods.

Dusty laughed out loud and hollered, "Loomeeyay doo joor!", and when Ralph laughed back and asked what does it mean, he said, <u>Somebody brung a torch & lit up the forest</u>.

We joked some more and chopped and had a good time, the three of us heaving big backswings, sliding the fist down the haft then sliding it up on the downstroke smooth as baby powder, the sun with beams & rays catching us through the shadows and our jokes bouncing back with echoes. We worked fast, crisscrossing each other, looking back at our work as the pathway started to shape up, zigzagging back and forth with me as the cleanup man chopping new growth or saplings too small for Ralph and Dusty to bother with. We stacked the brush & skinny logs along the side as we went. We were almost done when we first heard the trucks way up the dirt road, gearing down to make the steep grades then leveling off for straightaways. The sounds must've jumped Ralph's mind off what he was doing because he stopped behind me to listen with a big armload of tanglebrush just as I was heaving back for a swipe at a two-inch pine sapling. Dusty told me this because he saw the whole thing whilst taking a wipe of the face with his neck cloth. He said my axe caught Ralph in the back of the head and chunked in deep which I felt the jolt in my arms and the axe snatched out of my hands when he fell. Then I turned and saw him and the world froze up. My big brother; a boy who never had a chance to cash in his promises. He was laying like a Sunday cowboys & indians comic, my axe stuck deep in his head and no blood that I could see. As the trucks braked in and the men jumped out to join Dusty Broom who was on his knees seeing what could he do for Ralph, Mr. Roberson, the big boss, put his arm around my shoulder and patted me. "A kind boy," he said, looking over at Ralph. He patted me some more and said it again, twice, then he looked at me and said, "Maybe you are a jinks." It was the first I heard about jinks, but I have heard it plenty since. It is what other people call you when things you are in go wrong. When things they are in go wrong, they call it hard luck.

The deputy who came out told us it would be awhile before an ambulance could make it from Smith's Ferry, being deep woods and all, also meanwhile said there was no need to take me in because Dusty Broom had told the whole story and it was an accident. But tomorrow the sheriff would like to have a word with me.

Back then when I was young, I tried to be more than I was. Now I am trying to be all that is left.

That night I ran.

So long ago that was. Today I can't remember what Ralph looked like exactly, but now & then through the years I see a young boy and say <u>He looks a little like Ralph</u>. And when I smell something clean and soapy I say <u>That smells a little like Ralph</u>. And in the market sometimes or in a school yard when I am passing, a boy's voice calling, I say <u>That sounds a little like Ralph</u>. And even now, when I hear certain dogs barking and I listen hard, they aren't saying <u>Woof-Woof</u> or <u>Yap-Yap</u>, they are saying <u>Ralph-Ralph</u>. Once in awhile I miss him in the night like I did then, my brother.

So Father, I was twelve and had the sense to head South out of the cold, though still too small for my age that folks sometimes called me Runt or Twerp on the way. I put together a bundle carried under my arm or by the hand, hitching rides and hopping rigs, finding a soup kitchen now & then, also now & then a little job from folks not curious about a boy alone, only wanting the job done. Also I was not lonesome, being that when you are alone it is other people always finding ways to ask you things or need help that brings you into their life. That is how I met Tiny Bascom, called Tiny because of the opposite he was. Like fat men called Slim or tall people called Shorty. Tiny was fifteen and big as a zoo gorilla, on the road like me. He once told me that the best thing a man could do in his life is be a virgin with his wife till they died. I figure that's up your alley a ways, Father, right? You could give it a talk some Sunday, about the virgin I mean.

Tiny sang louder than train whistles, which I know from the trains that pulled out. He laughed and smiled all the time, easy to like but ridiculous; example, When he laughed he looked like someone with his foot stomped by a horse. And when he sang he forgot the words though the tune you could make out, always <u>Rumma-rumma-rumma zing-zang bang, Up the road, Knock on de door</u>. His favorite was Motown. "My momma was a singer-- <u>rumma-rumma- rumma</u>-- you ever hear of her? Patsy Hovis before she become a Bascom. Patsy Hovis from Detroit, that's Motown-- you ever hear of her? She almost sung on a record once."

The truth is, I never found much of a use for singing-- though folks have told me it richens the spirit-- and prefer music without words to stir it up.

I met Tiny at a railyard siding in the Spring outside Birmingham, Alabama. I saw he was on one knee wearing a gray mackinaw with brown stripes and his bundle on the side, trying to loosen up his foot which was caught between two tracks. He was black-handed from the deep bed of coke which he had to keep clearing off to get at the foot. It looked bad and must of hurt, but he wasn't yelling nor did I see a tear; no surprise, thinking he was a full-grown man from the size of him till he spoke. Then his voice gave it away that he was only a boy when he saw me.

"The shunt went off," he said. "Last night. I was sacked on the roadbed. Can you give me a hand?"

"You been stuck like that since last night? I was in the tool shed over there and never heard you holler. Why didn't you holler?" I said.

"Cops. Didn't want to ring in the cops. Help me out of this, will you?" Then I finally heard a groan.

"Looks like it hurts plenty--"

"Go get a pry bar from the tool shed. Hurry, feels like my foot may be broke."

So I did it and together we sprung him. Then it took the two of us to get his shoe off and the foot was swole, red as a Coca-Cola billboard. He didn't yell once.

"Does she hurt much? Can you walk?" I never saw such a thing.

He stuck out his hand. "You saved me, man, shake. My name's Tiny Bascom-- Darwin, but they been calling me Tiny since I outgrowed the crib."

"Andy Korso," I said, giving my woodcutter name when I shook his hand. "I am older than I look."

"That's good, because I will need somebody older than you look to lean on. I don't know if she's broke, but I know she won't take the weight." He stood up and put his arm around my shoulder and we limped him over to the tool shed, not far but getting nervous because we could hear switches banging up the line and a couple engines warming in the sidings.

"We can't stay here long," I told him. "The yard's woke up and the day crew will be here anytime."

"I know. I do railroads all the time. Railroads and inter-states, fastest way to everyplace. I know all about railroads."

His face was handsome but a little porky under the chin. I once heard Dusty Broom call it babyfat when he was raggin' on Ralph. His hair was long and needed a wash like the rest of him. "Well, you have to make up your mind fast. Either the road or a hideout." Then I figured I must be somewhere in the middle of this so I said, "I been running alone all winter, but it is not my first choice. I think there's cops want me up north. You run alone?"

He pushed himself back against some shovels for a rest and bobbed his head. "Wouldn't mind partnerin' though. You say your name is Angie?"

"Andy."

"Little as you are you don't have no trouble crawling in spaces, do you?"

That was the first I heard about spaces when you are on the road. But later I learnt how spaces are second to only food, and somebody who can double himself up or thin himself out is able to hide or sleep safer than others. There are spaces under bridges I been in that once I saw a cat and another a bird, all that would fit, so small the spaces were. Of course I knew this already but until you meet somebody the size of Tiny you don't give yourself a value for being small.

"If you want to come with me, you will have to wash up every day," I said.

He looked at me from his sore foot and made a little laugh. "Wash up? What are you sayin'?"

"Soap & water," I told him, "and a bath whenever there's a chance at it."

"A bath?"

"A bath. Your folks must of let you in on it. Right now you smell like you could drive a hog out of his pen. Who gave you your clothes, a dead man?"

Tiny rolled all this around in his head a minute. "We'll see," was all he said finally.

"Also you might as well know I'm a jinks. Accidents come after me," I said. "You will hear me call myself Frankie Farley or Greg Loomis once in awhile when I need to easy in or out of something. "Can you remember those names?"

"I can remember," he said, "and I don't believe in jinks. People mostly make they own luck."

We took a chance and stood in the shed for another hour then when traffic was high in the yard and on the road above us, up the bankment we went, me dragging the limping gorilla and sat on a grass swale right next to the highway. A million cars made wind passing us.

"How'd you get the lock off that tool shed last night?" Tiny said when he got his breath back.

"Chop," I said. "I am a logger, a woodcutter."

"Don't bullshit a new friend," he laughed. "You're a fly-weight. Loggers are big dudes. And where's your axe that you chopped the lock?"

"I used a rock. It is the way you do your wrist," I said.
"Don't give me that look, it's true. It is because you don't know how to do your wrist you can't believe it. It is a mystery to you. You know what a mystery is? It is the dark side of your brain, my brother told me, where God keeps everything you don't believe. Also an old logger name Dusty Broom told me whatever you ain't found out yet, that's a mystery. Big as you are, you should know that."

I had a shirt in my bundle lifted from a wash line passing through Dilly, Texas where stones follow you down the road to hop in your shoes, that I tore in strips and tied up Tiny's foot. He shook my hand when he watched me tear up a shirt like that and said I already did more nice things for him in two hours than anybody else in a lifetime, but he did most of the tying because he said good tying comes from practice and learning of it. I told him I did plenty tying myself in my time but not recently. He might of been a little sore at me from saying he had a mystery.

We hitched our way south to Oxmoor about ten miles from Birmingham and then had to quit because Tiny's foot hurt so bad. The rest of the day we hung up under a little bridge where he took off his shoe & sock and buried it in cool sand next to a still and sunny lake with bugs banging off the face of it and both fell asleep and never woke up even for dinner. Next morning, still dark, I told Tiny to stay put and I would see about breakfast.

"Yes, please," he said, "I am plenty hungry."

After a little walk around, I found a school and waited for the milk & roll truck which came when the sun balled up with red clouds behind, a raggy morning with rain in it I knew. I carried the food back to Tiny. He shook my hand again and said thank you over & over. "You already said Please, Tiny. When you say Please, you don't have to say thank you."

"I never heard of such a thing as breakfast from a school."

"Because you don't find schools in railyards and inter-states," I said, "where you spend all your time. You been so busy moving you never learnt the staying part."

He laughed and said I could learn him about the staying part and he could learn me about the moving part. "I done mostly day work-- stoop labor with the beaners and wetbacks." Then all of a sudden, before we even finished the milk, a storm blew in. It was a straight down dagger rain where the drops pop and break in a million water babies bouncing up so you can't see your feet in the mist of it if you are dumb enough to be walking out there. It is a noisy rain busting open on car roofs and cellar doors.

Tiny was glad to see it and stuck his foot out in it. He kept saying Ooh" and "Ahh" and "Man, that sure feels good," so much I was close to getting sick of it. One way to tell if a person and you click gears is getting trapped under a bridge or in a boxcar for a day, especially if it's raining. Some bugs come out only in the dark and the wet, if you know what I mean, so if you live through it and don't kill each other, you might be able to start up a friendship after all. In an hour the rain let up and I made him ball up his milk carton and wrapper from the roll and told him to dump it in a trash can.

"What? You expect me to bother little itty-bitty junk like this with a trash can?" he said.

"It's like washing up," I said, "or taking a bath. It's all part of getting old."

14

His eyebrows slid down and he said, "What are you talking about?"

"In the end, it's germs that get you, my brother Ralph told me. So if you wash up every day of your life they won't get you while you're young but wait until you're old and can't reach all the places. Same with trash. You are getting rid of germs. In olden days people left their trash laying around and you had disease and plaig so whole towns shut down and nobody left to bury the dead."

Tiny pulled back his neck and half shut his eyes in a smart alec look. "Did your brother Ralph tell you that too?"

"He did."

"Well answer me this-- ain't there germs inside trash cans?"

"Sure, that's where folks keep them."

"Then why should I go near one?"

I guess I had slipped up on that one and Tiny was not a dope, so I put on a sarcastic voice which I heard people do when they are losing. "Because they like it in there with their brothers and sisters and cousins. Would you leave family to go out and take a chance with strangers--"

"That is exactly what I done," he said in a regular voice, not mad.

"Excuse me," I said. "I didn't mean it as personal. Give me your trash and today I'll dump it for you, but you do your own starting tomorrow, okay?"

He bobbed his head like a winner to a loser and handed me his trash. Then a little later he put on his sock and shoe and tried out his foot and it was walkable, and then the rain quit while he was out in it. We decided he was okay to move on.

"Where to? he said.

"Where you headed?"

"Where are we now?"

I said, "Alabama."

"Then I was headed west."

"I already been west."

"Where?" he said.

"Oregon, Washington, Montana."

"Is that west?"

I said, "Very west, and also north some."

"I mean Arizona, Texas, stuff like that. I must go to Texas where they grow onions."

"Mississippi is west."

"Mississippi? It is?" he said.

"Right next door."

And like I learnt about Tiny Bascom in the days to come, he might not like the cards you deal him, but he will play out every hand. He said, "Mississippi's okay, I guess. I always wanted to rummel around New Orleans."

I said, "From where you're at, you must go to Mississippi to get to Texas anyway. You are that much closer is all."

"Mississippi gets me to Texas?" He shook his head, "They must of changed the maps."

We hitched and bummed and rode the rails, worked a few town jobs, picked orchard fruit, laid in the sun making pictures out of clouds. One place there was a little riot when the wetbacks hollered about the rotten food. When the sheriff said, "What about this slop you're feeding the help?", the owner said, "Oh yes, I will give them better food if you will make them legal." "Why then," said the sheriff, "if I did that, they wouldn't be illegal, would they?" And the sheriff went to the mayor who went to the governor, and the governor signed a paper for Exchange Students Field Work which made the rich owner richer whilst Jose got a finer grade of grits. Tiny said, "What Mississippi wants is not more voters, like some say, but more nut-houses."

For a couple months, Tiny Bascom was the nearest I ever had to a friend, and although he was poor at geography and needed reminding about baths and such, he knew the lessons of life clear through. He had dreams he swore he would never give up. "Someday, I will be a boss," he told me, "because bosses always sit in the shade."

"You should keep that to yourself," I said. "People don't like bosses."

"No," he said, "if you keep your dream a secret, why should anyone care of you give it up?"

On our last day together, he showed me something new: finding a toilet where you don't have to break a window or a lock and where they don't throw you out if they see you go in and you have to do it in an alley or behind a truck or in the park. In the woods is all right if you are on the run, except cleanup sometimes is a problem.

Still in Mississippi but on the road again we hit a little town called Oloh. Tiny's ankle never healed right from that first day we met and though he walked okay, there was a limp. Without a word he took us to the main street where there was a brick hut called City Hall, two office buildings, three empty stores, four parking lots and a Hamburger Jungle.

"How d'you know your way around these places?" I said.

He said, "The same dude built them all."

We sat down on a bench outside an empty store. "I'm hungry," I said.

"What time is it?"

I looked at my wrist and said, "Two hairs past a freckle," and Tiny's eyes popped open like he didn't know whether to laugh or cry, then begun smacking his palm with a fist, clapping his hands and slapping his leg whilst laughing himself down to a choke so the words come out like you had your hands around his throat.

"Two hairs past a freckle!" he gagged and laughed himself quiet except for a sob that rose up like a bubble now & then.

It was a lesson to me that all jokes are new if you never heard it, and <u>Two hairs past a freckle</u> is a girl's joke anyhow. "That's the first you heard of it?" I asked him. "You are on the road too much."

"What time is it for real-- I got to piss. And no jokes or I'll mess my shorts," he said, ready to laugh again but afraid of it.

I had to make a salute over my eyes with my hand to shade out the sun. "Well the big hand is on the nine and the little hand is on the twelve over there at City Hall."

He leaned his head on one side and looked where he saw me looking, "Uh-huh, twelve forty-five. Where are the lunch people?"

I said, "You must be an hour early for everything if you think that is twelve forty-five."

Tiny made a frown on his handsome face and scratched his chin roll. "I don't see so good sometimes, Andy, since the last time I got sold. I guess that is eleven forty-five, right? But my motto anyway is <u>Better early than always</u>," and he begun his dorky laughing all over again and said, "Get it? <u>Better early than always</u>? It's the backward way of <u>Better late than never</u>. I made it up myself!" Then he peed himself a little which sobered him up to a stop. "I got to piss," he said with a puppy look on his face.

"What d'you mean Since the last time you got sold?"

"Sold. Sold, like you sell something." He started walking with little short steps and yanked his jacket down in front to hide the wet of his pants. I could see he was headed for the Hamburger Jungle. "I can't wait no more."

"Somebody sold you?" My own natural steps kept up with his little ones. "How can somebody sell you? Who?"

"Well sure, my folks." Then he gave me a look, "You been sold, ain't you?"

"No, I never been sold. I know about slaves in the olden days, but today you sell dogs & cats, you don't sell people." We jumped the curb and crossed over the street. A beautiful gong hit twelve times from City Hall too loud to talk around, so I had to wait. Then I said, "Who bought you?" when we hit the sidewalk on the other side.

People started to hurry out of the office buildings, all headed to Hamburger Jungle and Tiny said, "Arabs."

"Cover your pee spot," I whispered to him. "We don't want folks to notice <u>nothing</u>."

He tug his mackinaw down again and said, worried, "She's covered as far as she'll go, Andy."

"Then hitch up your pants."

He did it and looked mighty pleased. "You are plenty smart for a runt."

"What Arabs?" I said.

But we reached the Hamburger Jungle where the windows were covered with pictures of monkeys in trees picking hamburgers off the leaves instead of bananas. Other pictures had them eating and chewing. Tiny looked at the pictures for a minute and shook his head. "That's the best sign I ever seen," he said, "they have even got real flies in it."

Then we went in and went to the bathroom where we took care of business and washed up, except Tiny only did a splash and a few hand shakes. I made him go back and take off his jacket and shirt and pump a real handful of pink soap under each arm and do his neck twice while he grummeled and complained all the time. "What is this, the Junior Prom?" he said.

"No, you would have to go to school a hundred years to make Junior," I said, "and who would be left to go to the Prom with you?"

Men came in & out of the men's room and one or two stared at Tiny splashing and making a mess but said nothing.

I said, "Tell me about the Arabs." I figured he would rather be talking than complaining.

"My mama called them Arabs, but maybe they was only gipsies. I myself think they were gipsies."

"Your parents sold you to the gipsies?"

Tiny squirted a big spot of pink soap in one hand off the soap machine and dumped it on his wet head and started to scrummel his hair, bent over with his eyes closed, all the time talking which gave his voice a shiver. "Sounds funny, don't it? Gipsies is supposed to <u>kidnap</u> you, not buy you-- everybody knows that. Expecially if you're bad. I been bad so much I guess my folks got tired of it and figured if the gipsies were out to kidnap me anyway, there ought to be some bread in it for them. Why not sell me?"

"You're some storyteller, Tiny," I said.

"No, it's true, I swear it every word. They beat me up so much, my eye busted. I got a plastic eye. You seen that, right? You must of noticed, didn't you?" He was getting loud.

"Quiet down and rinse out your hair. Your voice is yelling; you want to get us tossed?" The truth is, I became nervous in the stomach when he told about his eye. I never noticed, I never saw it. I wanted to say Straighten up this minute and let me see that eye!

Then I heard him laughing a little, burbling his words under the sink tap. "You are some dweeby dude, Andy. They was junkies is all."

I started a smile, "Your folks sold you to junkies?" Somehow, that made it a little easier in the stomach for me because junkies are in your every day living and not in books like gipsies.

"No, my <u>folks</u> was junkies. They sold me to their dealers. The selling part is true. I always ran away, and they always sold me again." Then Tiny got soap in his eye and flipped up from the sink, rubbing hard & yelling <u>Jesus, Jesus, Jesus</u>! He was twisting so much from the burn of it, I couldn't hold him straight so he slid on the soapy tile floor and flipped like a gym rat where he landed on his head with a thunky sound I knew was trouble, and when he hit, out pops his plastic eye in a looper that lands it near the door.

Some of the men coming in & out tried to take care of him. Another one said Call 911. When I heard the sirens pull up, I gave him a look and ran out of there, stepping over the eye. Tiny Bascom was getting to be a nice friend to watch out for my back, but big as he was, he could not buck my luck.

Frankie Farley

By the time I was twenty, Father, I finally looked my age. My feet put a lot of miles on those years with stories more sour than lemons. Met enough people for an army in subways, under bridges and even a tramp camp or few, but no friends stuck. How could they? Everybody in the world is on a ramble to a different place, and if you find you are on the same track with someone for part of it, don't ask for more. I came through hard luck to more hard luck yet made a comeback every time with no complaints, for Dusty Broom told me all the days you live are only practice for the last.

"What'll it be, Sir?" asks the counter girl.

"Coffee, and if you got some, a hunk of yesterday's bread," I said.

It was a tiny town called Locutan, gulf coast Florida between Fort Myers and Naples in a diner, raining hard, yellow slickers at all the tables, rubber boots some red some black, everything smelling a little fishy with sunfried men dark as char rubbing their beard, both hands in a napkin to get the wet out. A few women in the booths further back from the voices I could hear. The noise put me in mind of a slow boil in a pot on a stove. I could see some fishing boats rolling at a pier outside with soggy lines and everything on the drench waiting for the summer squall to run out.

"You're soaking wet," says the counter girl, only now when I look at her is not a girl but a woman way way past <u>girl</u>. Midsize, hair in a bun once blonde you could see is now muddy with a streak here & there. Built on the chunky side but looked solid though the face showed wrinkles.

"The train leaked," I told her.

"No train stops here, sonny."

"Well, how about a bus. A truck? A horse. How about a leaky horse?"

She poured coffee with her little finger out straight. There was no smile on her. "Drink that, then go in back and I'll bring you a towel." People called out <u>Waitress</u> from the booths and a fat man in overalls reached for her arm but she hunched around him. I saw two other waitresses busy on the run in & out to the short-order cook calling, "Bishop, is my turkey club-no-mayo ready?" and "Where's my cheese-steak, Bishop?" but people seemed to have an eye and favor this one. It was summer and the air conditioner was pounding, but steam lifted off the urns and soup pots and a haze filled the place from the heat of people.

I drank the coffee and it was fresh and good, then caught her staring at me from back of the pass-through where she was pointing me with her eyes and headjerk tilted over her shoulder.

"I am too busy for this," she said when I snuck past the noisy crowd at the counter and ducked under a flap on a hinge. Bishop, the short-order cook smiled and gave me a salute. He was clean cut with a new haircut and one gold earring. Then the waitress tossed me a towel and said, "Dry yourself, I have orders out there to serve," and sort of danced away on white rubber waitress shoes. The short-order cook pointed to the back with his thumb.

The towel was soft and clean like I picked up now & then when I took a job in housekeeping for a few days at a motel passing through some nice town. Mostly, the towels I use you must locate a place on the edge not as dirty as the rest. I was in a pantry so it was easy to find the washtub and lye soap for a scrub. Finding soap & water is another trick you must learn on the road and I never been shut out, though truth is there's a chip of soap in my bundle for emergencies. I have always tried not to get clean towels dirty for it leaves a bad impression on folks. She came back and saw me with my shirt off in the middle of my scrub and shook her head and I could see there was respect for my washup.

"My soul, you poor boy, you're as skinny as a rail."

"I'm sorry," I said, pulling the towel up for cover. "I needed a scrub."

"No, no, I don't mean to interrupt. You go on with your wash and I'll come back later."

So Father, that is how I met Grandy, Grandy Cumberhouse, the sweet & gentlest lady of my life. You might say she took my mother's place without neither of us knowing it or saying so, but had it grow on us till one day there it was. She reads the newspaper crime reports out loud every day and can see the end of peace & prosperity in all of it. She is afraid of things most people never give a minute to and just as likely come out with ideas that scratch a blackboard up your spine, but she don't know how to say <u>no</u> and takes the rewards other folks give you for that and never suffered for it that I can see.

She did come back later that stormy day and carried me home in a taxi with her where she lived next to a choked-up marina and tumbledown docks in a peeled paint sea shack that was once a bait house with a young dog who went nuts to see her. The taxi drove on dirt most of the way and I could see ruts in the road that was just wide enough for us, a road between water and water, made me scared of alligators. Back then I didn't know mosquitos killed more people than alligators on that stretch of coast. Then turned on to a run of blacktop past a dead & rusty gas station with busted windows and pumps knocked over, through the middle of a building started on one side of the road and ended on the other.

I turned around to look at that. "The street-- it runs right through that place."

The driver chucked with a tight laugh close to his chest. This laugh always means somebody knows something you don't. "Yeah, cost too much to tear 'er down," he says. He had a bony nose and wore a baseball cap & thick glasses. "County saved twenty thousand on that job, thanks to the mayor in office at the time. Good luck hung on him like balls on a goat-- pardon my French, Grandy. Had to fight Streets and Parks Beautification every inch of the way. No business sense, them people. The commissioners give him a certificate. You can see it right there next to the cab license on the back of my seat."

The waitress touched my hand and put a finger to her lips whilst pointing with a jab of her other finger at the driver.

I took a look at the license and the other papers and then all of a sudden got the hang of it. "I'm happy to be in your hack, your honor," I said.

"No," he said and shook his head. "Not no more. I am not allowed to succeed myself for mayor but only once. However, good luck holdin'," he knocked his head twice, "Taylor Binns is out of politics for the moment, but I got plans."

"Did you fence in the wyandottes?" said the waitress like in a hurry to change the subject.

But the driver didn't answer and when we jumped out, the waitress said, "Taylor is very touchy about politics. Most of his friends were on Streets & Parks Beautification and they haven't said word one to him ever since."

"What is wyandottes?" I choked up a whisper as we ran up a walkway.

She whispered back, "Chickens. He is raising chickens for extra money but they wander off."

The hack motor died before we got in the house which I could see though getting darker with clouds needed bigtime carpenter work. I heard a mighty big bark from some dog inside. We went back to the taxi under the waitress's bent & stringy umbrella just as the back wheels slid off the blacktop and set down in the muck up to the axle. Ex-mayor Binns got out & looked at things with his chin in his hand whilst thunder & lightning sissed like a cat in the squall. I believe he would be there still if I don't say, "Maybe you should call somebody."

"No phone," he says.

"You got a phone in the house?" I ask the waitress.

"Of course."

Then we all went in after the waitress stuck the dog in another room, a small house all on the same floor, and waited as he called and waited some more for the tow, listening to ex-mayor Binns talk scared about his life which with politics, cab driving and chicken raising up till this minute has been better than ice cream. "I hate to say it, Grandy, but maybe my luck run out."

Of course it did. Frankie Farley just came to town.

"So, you are Frankie Farley," she said, turning me around in front of her like I was on skates. The dog backed off to one side, maybe scared of somebody that didn't smell like fish.

"I am Grandy Cumberhouse and the pup is Valerio. I'll tell you why that is-- I mean his name being Valerio, if you're interested." Her voice made me think of feathers and fresh cotton.

The tow truck, run by Taylor Binns' brother-in-law named Rudy, yanked the taxi out of the muck easy enough but could not turn around on the narrow blacktop with the taxi in tow. Neither could he unhook, turn around & rehook from the taxi's other end because there was no room on the blacktop to get to the taxi's other end once it had been sucked out of the mud. They scratched their heads trying to figure how to hook up the right way and scolded at each other in the rain as Grandy and me dried off, watching from the front window. In ten minutes or so she got fed up and stuck her head out the door and yelled.

"Taylor, see if the cab will start."

The ex-mayor rose up his hand to shut up his brother-in-law and yelled back, "What say, Grandy?"

"Start - the - cab!" she hollered loud as she could.

Taylor Binns bobbed his head and opened his mouth to let the idea in. He got in the cab which started right up, made a tight fivepoint turn and shot down the road the way we had come. The brother-in-law stood in the rain, maybe waiting for the cab to come back with an Okay or a high-sign or something but soon got the understanding of it. Ex-mayor Binns left him behind to do what he could with a rainy evening.

Valerio must of got fed up too, for he said Aboo-Roo-Roo! and zanged out the open door past Grandy making for the tow truck man who saw the business end coming at him through the rain at 50 mph. He fumbled up into his truck and made the gears cry getting out of there. The dog tried to shift course but he was in the muck by then and slid twenty feet on his cork in a sitting position like you see a young pup do on a rug when the worms go at his bung. Then he circled around his tail three or four times trying to see with his nose what harm he did to himself.

25

Grandy shut the door and shook her head. "Don't grow up to be a fool, Frankie, though it is probably in the blood of all boy babies the minute they are born. Dogs too, I think," she said with a sweet grin, "boy dogs."

"Beg your pardon," I said, "but <u>dumb</u> ain't marked boy or girl." Then to ease it up-- for I felt this was too soon in her house to say my own opinions of things-- I said, "Your dog is a hound."

She must of excused my bad manners because she took her end of the conversation without a hitch and flung it back. "Part. Most part maybe. Dropped off here by an Eastern European gentleman who happens to be the county animal warden. He adds to his income by selling-- against the law as you might imagine-- promising pups he picks up. Can't say his doubleyoos but must say vees in their place and suggested the dog's name begin with that familiar sound. <u>Villie Vonka</u> he believed, would do it. It would hurry the onset of bonding, he said. Well the dog never got the feel for that name and we settled on Valerio, the name of an old, old friend." Her voice dropped, came out sad, but no tears.

My eyelids shut for a minute till I heard myself snore and my head kept bending down my neck which sprung a yawn. "I only been here a few hours, Grandy, but I can see your town has got a flavor to it."

Now she smiled and let me know she liked the idea. "Locutan? Yes, yes I think so. Over the years, many interesting people have found the road to Locutan. I was a school teacher myself when I first arrived. We had a doctor once, and a dentist too, but he discovered that the natives had all their own teeth in the healthiest condition that he'd come across in an area nine miles square. <u>Locutan teeth</u>-- it's a well-known concept that the regional health authorities once promoted as evidence of a curative water supply. But I've seen enough people at the diner to know otherwise. It's the permit. I've seen permit fishermen ninety years old who've never had a cavity. Why, I've seen permit fishermen ninety years old who've never had bad <u>breath!</u>"

"Hold on, Grandy, I'm fallin' out. Mind if I have a sleep? If I find work, I'll look for a place later on. Maybe tomorrow. Or," and I yawned there, "it's the road again."

She was not ready to stop. "We had a dermatologist-- Emanuel Zorsky. We called him Manny, Manny the Dermatologist. He said he became a dermatologist because there are no midnight emergencies in dermatology. They didn't tell him how ugly it would be. He said other doctors deal with patients who look normal with diseases on the inside. His, the opposite."

I woke myself twice from snorfles in the middle of her stories. The last I remember, she was saying, "Sleep, yes sleep, Frankie Farley," and smoothed my hair and steered me to a couch where I hit the cushion and out.

*

Well Father, there was no crime in Locutan back then with mostly empty streets and hungry cats on the docks and bingo the only sport in town. Like I said, I was twenty when I first came, ready for growing. I stayed longer than other places I been for it was too hard to leave Grandy Cumberhouse behind to do for herself, even safe as the town was. The change came when the mystery lady with the slanty eyes showed up. You know her well now Father, the newspapers calling her HoHo Murn. She is the reason I stayed, and maybe also why I finally left. I will tell about her in the right place for it if you have not already been bonkered out from all the TV and magazine trash.

Back then folks left front doors unlocked, car keys in cars, carried cash in the open, trusted their children to be left alone outside whilst they went shopping, and did favors for strangers. The storekeepers kept accounts in their heads and the commercial boats weighed their own catch when they came in.

But that's all changed now as the world has leaked itself into everybody's life, is what Grandy says-- leaked itself into everybody's life. Human crime and devilment follow people, she says, and the only safe place is a place where no people are. The North & South pole maybe, and wherever the hottest place on earth is on its hottest day. When there are only two people left in the world, one will find a way to abuse the other and when only one is left, he will abuse himself, Grandy says.

Between the time I first showed up starved for a hunk of stale bread and met her at the diner that rainy day-- between then and now the people in town have changed, the feel of the town changed with them, yet watching it all, Grandy stayed the same. She will still save drowned cats & dogs like me and spend more of herself than she's got in the bank-- "My life is overdrawn," she said more than once-- and never an eye on the risk. Like I already told you, in the morning paper she will read the bad news from everywhere out loud and make grief in herself for folks she never met.

*

I been going back to those old days in my head. When you are young, your troubles last a day. They look like serious troubles to you because you can't see anything but what's standing right in front, and they must pass to make room for what is waiting tomorrow-- something else standing in front. When you grow up, trouble is an ocean with things in it pull you to deep water and then push you under. Nothing stands in front, nothing stands clear alone for you to see and then you know that all the days you live and things you do are connected to each other. Nothing passes and tomorrow only dumps more ballast on. Life is chains, webs & nooses. It is the reason grownups call the "old days" simple. Is it because horse & wagon is simpler than jet planes? Or because jet planes dragged a net through factories and wars and politicians and the dirt they make on the way to be jet planes? No; I decided it is grownups who were simple in the old days because they did not grow up yet. Now they are grown up and don't like the mess they carried in with them. Old days, new days-- don't mean nothing.

I didn't know where I was and didn't know I was yawning until one of them squeaked and woke me up the next day. My eyes peeped out under a sheet and saw a sight. Doodads, in color loud enough to burn your eyeballs. Little shiny horses and

28

dancing fairies, fish, trees with fruit, boats & cars, jelly jars full of marbles, teeny clocks, ashtrays, pearly shells, bowls with pencils in them, pictures in little frames with flowers on them-- everything setting on big tables, little tables, boxes and shelfs. Also I smelt cooking.

"You are awake; good," I hear Grandy say. "The rain has stopped, see the morning."

I never like people to be up & awake ahead of me for it is possible to lose advantage if you are not careful where you slept. "Sure. Thanks. I see the sun. I'll wash up and clear out-- ten minutes, FIVE minutes is all. Thanks for the flop, Miss Grandy--"

She was at the open door and the sun blared out my sight when I turned into it, and when things began to come back slow & furry she looked like she must of looked young. I saw a face like a heart with big dark eyes up high on a straight neck and lemon hair, easy turning my way so as it stopped my breath & made me swallow hard.

"Nothing of the sort, Frankie. You'll wash up and have a decent breakfast."

"Breakfast," I said like it was a word in another language. "I been smelling it."

"Bacon and eggs, grits, biscuits and gravy and all the milk you want! And a sleep after, if you like. Your clothes are cleaned; in the laundry room."

"Oh, no sleep, no more sleep," I said like a gargle in my throat, tripping on my sheet wrapped around me on the way to the bathroom.

It was the best breakfast I ever ate till then. She stuffed me with food and talk, and I talked back. In the kitchen was cabinets with painted flowers & animals on the front, also like the doodads in colors that make you blink. And in the cabinets, glasses with gold rings around and dishes, green, blue, yellow and white. I began to get the idea of "good company" that I heard many a lonely lumber man say in those cold winters I left behind with only theirself to talk private things to.

I said, "There is a quarter million acres Ponderosa pine ready for harvest in a state I worked where none but a few knows of."

"But you know, right Frankie? You are telling me a secret?"

Her voice was now a play-voice, like happy to see a new game started.

"If I was to let on, there would be an axe waiting next time I set foot in the woods."

"Oh come," says Grandy, "who would harm you for-- for lumber?"

"You can't guess how many houses is in a quarter million acres. I heard of more than one logger sent down the flume lips sewed together from too much talk. It is more money than you can write down on one piece of paper."

"You're trying to frighten me," she says over her shoulder going to the sink with dishes.

Right then shoved up in the clear an idea stuck somewhere my tongue couldn't reach since she took care of me yesterday in the diner-- Grandy Cumberhouse could not be frightened. She was planted solid, eyes around her head, ready with words to lick the world. It must be a good feeling to be like that. "No, but I been places and seen things in twenty years."

"And now-- and, and now you are-- in-- LOSHutan!" She sneezed a couple more times in her hand, little fricker-sneezes with a breath on the end, then shut her eyes and pulled her front lip down a minute. "Ahh," she says, "pardon me. Allergies. "I was never bothered with this when I lived in the city." She made little honks in a tissue, wiped back & forth then patted. "In the mornings mostly, onshore breeze. We're almost surrounded by swamps and forest."

I said, "I never had it, allergies, but it don't seem too high a charge for country life."

Water sprung in her eyes and Grandy sucked in air for another sneeze, but it didn't come. "You don't like cities?"

"No, no not that, I don't figure it is like or not-like. Cities is a good place to put all those buildings, I think. There is just not enough for a man to do in cities."

She put on a sweet smile then and I was happy to be entertainment. "It is an unusual opinion, Frankie. Now you go get dressed while I finish the cleanup. Your clothes are folded on top of the dryer."

When I got into my shirt and pants I smelt like candy. "Last night I saw there is repairs to do on the outside of your house. I owe you a day's work," I told her, "and I am handy with tools."

She was wiping up the sink, squeezing sponges and snapping a towel and didn't answer for a minute. Then she spanked the curtain on a window above the sink and straightened the pleats. Through the window I saw smoky clouds coming fast from the northeast. "All right, it's a fair exchange," she said. "I'm on the late shift this week anyway."

Her last remark did not mean anything to me except maybe she would be around to keep an eye on me. Then she said, "There's petty cash in the old laquered tea can up on the shelf by the sink-- see it? After you work off whatever you decide you owe me, I will pay you two-fifty an hour for other work you do around here. Keep track of your own hours and take the wages out of the tea can. All right?"

Grandy lived maybe two miles out of town without a car to get to work. At 3:30, me out front punching aluminum sinker nails into new beveled siding, up drove the cab, clean washed and shined with Taylor Binns looking likewise. Loose tappets made his motor go clickety-clack. Today he wore no baseball cap or glasses and his hair was combed with a high handmade wave up front. For the first time, I saw his face, made strong with smiler muscles. "Hey Junior, how's it hangin'," he yelled up the walk, first making sure Grandy is not around. He rapped on the horn twice with the heel of his hand off a stiff arm. "That a straight claw hammer you're usin'?"

I held it up for him to see. "Curve claw."

"You want a straight claw for that job, son. Ripping hammer, twenty ounce."

"I like the cheek on this one-- fat poll and crowned face," I yell so loud in Grandy's ear as she came out the screen door right then, she gave a scared jump.

"My word, Frankie," she said, like scolding. Her waitress dress white as angel wings. "You want to blow my eardrum?" Valerio tried to sneak out before the door closed and latched but she nagged him back in and his ears drooped.

"Sorry," I said and could not stop a laugh, which she laughed back at, "it is my manners."

Getting in the cab, she hollered, "Come by the diner at seven for dinner. It's part of the deal. Mr. Binns here will pick you up."

The ex-mayor made another five-point turn on the little street like the night before and pulled to the mud shoulder again. "Hope you're usin' cedar." When I shake my head yes he yells, "Hope it's sawed edge-grain-- flat-grain will warp and peel on you."

"Your tappets is loose," I hollered just when he gunned away.

Sawed-edge grain, flat grain. I been on this mosquito-bite job the last six hours, I am thinking, ordered the goods, took delivery, tore off the old siding and half finished setting in the new. I will make my own advice without the bother of others.

I finished in time, washed up and was ready for the cab when it came. Mr. Binns talked all the way into town and I didn't have to join except for head-bobs & grunts to keep him going.

*

"You will find him at the sluice on Taylor Binns's place. He will be working on his airboat, no doubt. That thing is a miracle, I tell you. Made it himself from old oil drums, decking off wrecks he dug out of the phragmites and a propeller from a B-26 airplane went down in the forties. Both coasts in the state were Army Air Force territory fifty years ago," Grandy said. "'One a day in Tampa Bay,' they used to say about the B-26. After the war he got permission to ride with the Army Engineers when they dredged the harbor and they pulled out thirty-some wrecks. Crew's bones still in a few. He goes out with them once in awhile even now and finds things all the time, but I don't know where he got the motor." Then she pointed at a kettle with a wire handle on the stove. "It's hot, and he'll be wanting it for lunch before it cools down. You'll need to wear gloves." Grandy had a rag around her hand squeezing something on it from a plant. Her face crimped up from the hurt of it.

32

"What's his name again?"

"Esau. Philpot. Esau Philpot."

"How come you are making his lunch?"

She looked at me like this was not a question for anything to do with me, but her good manners made her answer. "Esau usually takes his lunch at the diner like most other folks, but once in awhile he gets occupied and Mr. Binns asks me to put something up." Then maybe because I still looked stupid, she said, "It's a business arrangement."

"Say again how far up the road is it?"

"It's just next door, Frankie, where Mr. Binns keeps his chickens. You go out to the road and turn right--"

"How far to the <u>house</u> on the property? How far to the <u>sluice</u>. Don't forget I am a country boy and I know what 'just next door' can mean."

"You could've been there and back by now, for Heaven's sake. Take your work gloves and keep the kettle away from your legs. "

Grandy's voice notched up and she was starting to cluck at me with her patience run out, so I said, "What happened to your hand?"

Right away she forgot about me and leaned her head with a puzzle in her eyes. "I burned myself; I <u>burned</u> myself. On the kettle. I haven't had a kitchen burn since I was a child. I can't understand it."

I said, "Last time, I swear, what's his name again?"

"Esau, <u>Esau</u>, for Heaven's sake."

"I never heard a name like that for a black man," I said.

Grandy gave me a look of misunderstanding. "Now you have."

He was whanging at a fifty-five gallon steel drum with a 16 pound sledge when I first saw him. It gave me pleasure to see he knew how to sling it; on the angle over a shoulder with one hand sliding for control and no rebound to come up and mash your eyeball. I was breathing so deep I sucked a bug in my throat and I bent down to cup a handful of squish from the water around my ankles. Of course I heard him way before I saw him, jumping big birds with long legs up in the air out of the marsh with each

33

whang. Every time a <u>shoosh</u> and a scrub-board sound from the flutter, and feathers like a busted pillow floating. You can tell farm land from fish land down here by the size of bird's legs. Farm land has stubby-leg birds, but fish land birds have long legs because you can onestep off a hard ground stand of saplings and find yourself knee high in muck. You can drop your axe to wipe your face and hear it sucked under forever. You can lose your shoes right off your feet only one step past a road shoulder. That is why fish land birds have long legs down here. But they tell me the orange juice is sweet.

I began to hear a sound like a million squirking truck tires a mile away. It was the ex-mayor's chickens, but not loud enough that Esau did not hear me gargling air, for the whanging stopped and a dark voice in a barrel hollered, "Lunch?"

I tried to yell Lunch back at him but was too dry in the swallow. I tried again and coughed out the bug. I hear him holler, "Mind the gator."

It was important news and leaped me ahead faster than the kettle wanted, sloshing me some with hot gravy. In a minute, I was on dry land next to him deep-heaving for air and holding my soaked and steamy pant leg off my scalded skin between a pinch of the fingers. Off to the side and back toward the barn was a neat-looking man digging with a shovel who was built from here like Bishop the short-order cook in the diner the first day I met Grandy Cumberhouse. He picked up his head and gave me a salute.

"Mind the lunch," Esau said and sat himself on a wide shiny stump next to the oil drum he must of been whanging, for it was all but flat. He was taller sitting than I was standing next to him with shoulders a yard wide. His arms were clubs you could beat off a bear. Three chickens with stripes pecked at the ground nearby to us.

I said, "What gator?"

"Set the pot down, son. Set the pot down and splosh some water on them trousers. Take care of your shank before it blisters up. You a jumpy young fella, ain't you?"

I stood where I was. "You got a gator here, or is this a joke on the new boy in town?"

He reached for the kettle and I let loose of it, for his hand was big as a baseball glove. Also, my leg had the stiff pucker feeling you get off a burn.

He had an eye on me and read my mind. "Over there in the trough. Clean water."

I took a step, then said, "That is for horses."

"Won't hurt them none," he said and smiled with a wide open mouth I could see a tooth missing at two o'clock. He studied as I bathed and breathed easy from the cool of it, then he said, "You want to stop now. You will blister tomorrow. Come by and I will make a poultice then."

While I rolled up my pants he stuck a finger in his ear and waggled after an itch. Then he scratched under his armpit and watched his foot swinging off his crossed leg. His face took looks of puzzlement, foolishness, meanness and sly, sweet as cupid yet not sure there is a God. This is how I met Esau Philpot without hearing him say his name or me saying mine.

"What is in the pot?" he said.

"Grandy made you chicken."

He took the lid off and breathed in deep, looked after the three striped hens which were scratching by a fencepost, made a happy sigh and said, "The gospel bird." Then he started in to eat, which was the right thing to do.

*

"Frankie, listen here to this," Grandy says. She has got the sniffles. Valerio is sleeping under her chair but wakes up when she coughs now & then.

"Where did you catch that cold at, Grandy," I say.

"Doctor Upperjoe's. I can't understand it, Frankie. I've always thought of myself as the healthiest and least accident-prone person in the world. But recently--" Grandy let her voice seep up into her thoughts before she went on again. "Went there to get a shot and a dressing for my burn," she wags her hand at me with a nice bandage & tape on it, "and half the fools in town were there coughing and sneezing their brains out. It happens every year this time, the bug comes to Locutan and folks wind up sick. They should know enough to stay indoors, first sign. Now listen to this and don't try to put me off."

I say, "You burnt your hand and went to the doctor and come home with a burnt hand and a cold. Next you will go to the doctor for your cold and come home with split liver & mangels."

But she did not fall for it and gave me a look for me to listen.

I say, "I got to clear off the breakfast stuff so I can get up and finish the shingles," for I know what is coming. Outside all is slosh and peep and purr, morning sounds for animals in a world of water and marsh, and I can see out the window the early fog tail off the basin where boats are hid in it, knocking piers with the men hollering, getting ready to head out after fillay of bass & baked flounder. My own leg smarts under the blister that showed up in my sleep. I keep it hid from Grandy.

"Leave the dishes for later; I want you to hear this. Some folks think newspapers are all taradiddle, but they are fools-- the news comes from some where doesn't it? This is from Philadelphia. You must've passed through Philadelphia on your travels." She is dressed in a pretty robe with her hair combed and her waitress shoes on because she has the early shift today at the diner. She holds the morning paper out in front of her and reads to me out of it. "Number of Homicides By Strangers Increases. In California, a 3-year-old girl is shot to death by gang members because the car she is in made a wrong turn. In Detroit, a 19-year-old who had fought his way back from cancer is shot to death by a teen-age girl who wanted cash. In Newark, a college freshman is killed on her porch by a bullet intended for someone else. A few days later, a Philadelphia police officer is shot in the head in an unprovoked attack. Within a week, he is dead. Justice Department crime data show that the proportion of persons slain by family members has declined sharply while the number of people killed in robberies and by unknown persons has grown in the last 3 years."

I cluck my tongue and shake my head the way she likes when she is mad at the newspaper, "That is sure a terrible thing, Grandy."

"Sit down, I'm not finished. The world is getting to be a sewer all over. Look here, in the local news. Peter Paul

Baranski Dead in Canal. Peter Paul Baranski, 64, prominent Fort Myers businessman died when his car plunged into Canal 31L near Naples yesterday. His remains were identified by his son Harry, CEO of Appleton and Murren Import-Export, Fort Myers. Sheriff's Deputy Willard DeSoto said, 'It looks like brake failure right now. Mr. Baranski had just took the car into the shop two days ago for brake problems.' See, Frankie, it's got down to your neighborhood mechanic. Nobody can be trusted to do good work. It's shoddiness and self-interest and greed. Now listen to this from Nairobi-- you know where Nairobi is, Frankie?"

With my head ducked in my shoulders and my eyebrows up, I say, "Overseas?"

"You can say that," she bobs her head. "It's in Africa, and it says Rising Mob Violence Dims Hope In Kenya. A drunk staggers through a vegetable market and squashes some tomatoes. Shoppers drop their packages and kick him to death. In the same week, a man is accused of stealing a goat. Neighbors pounce and kill him with clubs. A hat is stolen off someone's head. Kill the thief. A bus is involved in an accident. Beat the driver to death. A boy dies in a hospital. Stab the grandmother, she is a witch. Mobs now take it upon themselves to enforce social norms. Sometimes it is with extreme cruelty: a schoolteacher is dragged from her home, pinned on the ground and circumcised." Grandy stops to look at the ceiling, for a picture of it I think.

And my mouth is open now, from attention. "It is awkward to talk about, Grandy, but that part about the schoolteacher can not be right."

"It's right enough, Frankie. You'll find out about such things later, along with other things. Just remember, you don't have to do everything you know." She picked up her coffee cup but it was cold and she made a sour face. "People find a way when they're crazy. Life was always cheap when you had to kill with a rock or a club or a knife, but it's even cheaper now because guns are cheaper and drugs are cheaper and children who have toy brains play with them like they are toys. Then they say they're sorry-- that is, <u>sometimes</u> they say they're sorry, but never never do they feel guilty."

I say, "What does it matter <u>what</u> they feel?"

Grandy stretches, gets up and starts for her room to change. Then she turns around to me frowning like grownups are supposed to do. "Listen to me, Frankie, feeling sorry is easy. You're probably sorry for something ten times a day. I know I am. Then tomorrow we start over. Being sorry is only regret and regret blows away sooner than later without doing a thing about it. But <u>guilt</u>, guilt stays; and it stays until you <u>do</u> do something about it. Guilt makes more decisions for you than you can imagine. Always remember, guilt is stronger than regret."

Grandy knows what she is talking about, all right, for sometimes when I am not ready, my brains bring my brother back to me and then nothing, not the woods or river or mountain, not a meal when I am hungry or sleep when I am wore can chase him back inside my heart.

*

Esau swooshed a sharpened chicken quill around a bunged aluminum cup with his moonshine in it, then sat down on his shiny tree stump and popped my blister where my leg in his hand looked like a spruce twig. He got up and went and poked a long stick in the ground fifty feet off, where the solid gravel of Taylor Binns's drive gave way to marsh. Every now & then he stooped and grabbed a handful of mud which he fingered through and smelt and finally carried some back to lay on my burn. Right away the itch and ache of it calmed down.

I said, "What is this stuff?"

He tossed out the moonshine from his cup then poured himself a clean one from a jelly jar. "Can't say. I know it when I see it, that there's a fact." He stuck his finger in his ear and waggled his hand which I now figured was some kind of habit.

"Well, I want to thank you for taking care of it," I said. "I finished shinglin' Miss Grandy's shed roof this morning and it was a pain on my leg up there when the sun came out. That's the

38

last of it, though, the shinglin'. Now her place is fit to live in. You some kind of handyman for Mr. Binns? Is it all right if I call you by your name?"

He said, "Son, I once went to a preacher for smoothin'-out, and after I told him my sad story, he said I must repent. I said how, and he said I must say ten Hail Marys and ten Yo Mommas. That was him laughin' at me. Then he asked me what I do and is it all right if he call me by my name." He sat down on the stump. "Since then, I never give leave for it. If you must call my name, you do it on your own."

"I mean no harm," I said.

"Miss Grandy is good in her heart," he said and bobbed his head with that wide open smile of his. "And she seem to like you. Folks been sayin' you don't mind hard work. That's good, I can tell you. Man go forth to his work and do his labor till the sun go down. My mama always told me that when I slacked off- - it's from the bible. My name is Esau, what everybody calls me. I don't work for Mr. Binns, he rent the barn and coops for his chickens. I own this place."

With those last words Esau went up ten points. It is weak-minded and small-hearted of me, I know, and nobody can say why that is so, but it is. Wasn't anyone taught it to me but I learnt it: a man who only works is less than a man who owns. "Locutan has sure got a little bit of everything," I said, and was about to ask him about the chickens when he got off his stump and stuck his hand out for a shake. His shadow put me in deep shade.

"Pleased to know you, Mr. Frankie. I already talked to my boy about you. Dexter; Dexter Philpot, the best finish carpenter in the county. Six months he been lookin' for a prentice, and when I told him about you, with the knack of it born in you, he say Send him around. I spoke to Miss Grandy too, and she say she can spare you the chores for a couple weeks till Dexter finish the church steeple job. Start tomorrow at seven, church steeple, middle of town. It is a Baptist church but mostly Methodists come-- a few Piscopalians maybe. In this town, even Methodists is Baptist."

"I am not looking for extra work, Esau," I told him.

He waggled his ear-finger again and said, "Accordin' to Miss Grandy, it is a manner of ownin' what already been gave to you. She said you would know what that means and wouldn't mind the work. It is three dollars an hour work."

I knew what Grandy meant. She meant working off the value of a job you were paid in advance for. I started out with her by sleeping and eating first, then choring it off the next day, and it is a way where you will always be a day behind. That is all right with me, for I cannot ever pay off how she took me in. If she wanted to lend me out, I would go; still, I never had to sell off my free choice of it for three dollars an hour.

Esau turned away and put his hand to his eyebrow for the sun to give a look down the road. Then I heard what he was looking for-- loose tappets rolling fast up the tarmac and knew the ex-mayor was here.

Taylor Binns hit the drive and cut his wheels which sent a fan of gravel-spray twenty feet before he skidded to a stop and out of the taxicab with a THUNK of the door standing in front of us with the biggest fish I ever saw in his arms cradled like a baby. His eyes was wild and his baseball cap on sideways. "Hey Esau, hey Junior-- what you think of <u>this</u>!"

"Wahoo!" Esau yelled.

"Yahoo!" I copied his wonderment.

Esau showed me his grin and said, "No son, it's a wahoo. The fish be a wahoo--" and then helped Taylor Binns set the fish down on the shiny tree stump.

The ex-mayor let out a big relief in his breath. "Forty-nine pounds," he said. "Full moon last night, and there's loads of bonito out there. They're takin' bonito. Kings and tinker mackerel too. One of the men said he hooked a fifteen pound tunny and a wahoo came under and snatched it off. They're feedin' on everything."

"Last week it was goggle-eyes and ballyhoo," said Esau. "Somebody said down the diner they was even takin' dolphin."

"That's why I went out this morning," Taylor Binns said. "I couldn't let a run like this get past me. Why, it's been five, six, seven years since wahoo this size been seen on nearshore reefs."

Esau took some of the excitement. "They be fishin' along the dropoff," he said to me. "Two hundred to four hundred feet like that," he snapped his fingers under my nose, "the bottom falls away. Baitfish likes the dropoff."

"I used a double-hook rig with 7/0 hooks," Taylor Binns said. "Wire leader onto 30 pound test line. This one," he bobbed his head at the fish on the stump, "he dumped 250, 300 yards of line on his first run."

"Thirty-two ounce sinker?" said Esau.

"Twenty-four. It was calm this morning. Went down 50, 60 feet with two baits and put a trailer on the surface about 200 feet behind. What's Junior doin' here?" Taylor Binns said.

"I fix him up a poultice for a gravy burn he got yesterday," Esau answered him.

The ex-mayor came over and took a look at my leg. He stuck out his lips and sloped his eyebrows together whilst bobbing his head and pointing at the job Esau did. "Alligator shit-- better'n anything you can get in a drugstore. You better believe it, Junior."

That night Taylor Binns and Esau grilled the wahoo over hickory chips I chipped with an old axe Grandy found in her shed. We were all together with beer and laughing and joking, full of good, fresh food and being there like a family. Neighbors stopped by, for there was plenty.

3

Dexter Philpot

I am not easy in high places. Not because way-high is scary, but because you are there for everybody to see, a mile in any direction. It is a hangover from my road days when I hid under bridges and under boxcars. A church steeple is way-high, and when I got to the job I saw two raw hands up on top pulling off the last rotten plywood sections. They scrummeled around like rafter rats through the openwork, hefting prybars to test the wood whilst the boss called instructions. Dexter Philpot was all business, soft in the voice like his daddy, even taller but skinny with a shaved head and gold chains around his neck. At seven in the morning he was already on the scaffold, a hundred feet up, laying out a rafter with seat cuts & plumb cuts.

When he got sight of me, he called, "You must be Mr. Frankie. Come on ahead, I will show you hammer, I will show you nail," then bust out laughing like he heard a joke on TV. It made me wonder if the next two weeks would be job talk or circus.

The scaffold was nine storeys, all ladders and rails, paint chips flying off the rust every time I shook her, and by the time I got to the top, Dexter Philpot had my tools and bib set up and ready to strap on. He stuck his hand out like his daddy did the day before. "Very pleased to know you," he said.

"Likewise, I am sure, though the air is mighty thin up here," I opened my charmer smile on him.

"I am glad to point out it is thin because the dust and bugs and town junk is what makes it heavy down below, Frankie. Pure air be always thin, same as pure food be always light."

This was my first lesson taught by Dexter Philpot. No, I would like to change that-- it was not a lesson; lesson is too loaded for the way Dexter said things. They were point-outs, not lessons: they always go, I would like to point out, or D'you mind if I point out, or Please let me point out, or It is my pleasure to point out. And after he pointed-out, Dexter would come up with a sample of it that looked like good sense but was always dead wrong, like <u>pure air be always thin, same as pure food be always light</u>. Maybe when you are a boss, you get to think your words should <u>be</u> lessons.

I said, "I'm not trying to tell you how to run your business, but why don't you have a safety harness on your boys?" The rafter rats were hanging off the plate like monkeys and poking for termite wood.

"Oscar and Justin?" he said. "Watch 'em, surefoot as mount-ain goats. You go out and buy safety this and safety that, you must price up your bid. Pretty soon you be losin' contracts."

"I would hate to be the one to call up next of kin on your jobs," I said. I swung out onto the steeple with a heavy exten-sion cable that I tied one end around my waist and the other around a tension web of the roof truss.

Dexter Philpot-- who had not lost a stroke with saw, plane or hammer the whole time we jawed-- he had a big laugh on what I said about next of kin and also the way I tied myself to the steeple. He kept his eye on all of us and on the job too which cuts the danger of it, for a good manager ups your confidence.

A few days later, we had to take off the whole top when Oscar and Justin dug into termites. They were in half the rafters and trusses, and since you cannot paint over termites, the four of us spent the next day reinforcing the plates all around to make ready for a new roof. Down on the ground, Dexter rubbed his head and looked up at the job. He said, "I give the church a penalty clause when I signed up. This be settin' us back some. We got ten days to put in rafters, trusses, decking and new surface, otherwise every day extra, money come off the top."

I said, "We could leave out the purlins and save a day."

He shook his head, "We don't leave out nothin'."

"Then we will do it in ten days," I said, and he smiled. I cannot give the reason for it, but that smile was like money too.

*

"You must of heard it-- screelin' and honkin' and splashin' and hootin'. And gators, they can roar like a tiger if you rile 'em, you know that? Nighttime in the glades ain't a place you be wantin' to take your girl," said Dexter. We were laying under trees next to the church after lunch. Oscar and Justin snored and snorfled in the shade.

"I heard it. It sounds like freeway traffic in Birmingham, Alabama." It was only half a joke, but Dexter laughed like I meant the whole thing to be one. There was too many snaps and water gurgles for me-- too many green things turned black-- too many squeaks and chokes like little animals on a last breath. I heard there is a monster which turns to mist.

"It is traffic, all right," he said, "the first traffic, original traffic, God's traffic, I like to point out. He made the world, they tell me, but nobody said he made it safe."

I was looking up at the job, "When will the sheet copper guy show up?"

"When we call him. It is Ramon Taborda-- you know him? If he's sober and brings a helper, it's a one day job. Drunk, we're in trouble. No helper, take him two days. Let's get on up there; wake up them sleepers-- hey Justin! Hey Oscar!"

Dexter told me Justin and Oscar were from the orphanage up St. James City on Pine Island, a little town across from the mouth of the Chatahootchie River, not far. They were both sixteen, one light, one dark, one skinny, one soft, one smart, one not so much, both dressed for the job, clean, long-haired but neat cut with rubber soles so's not to slip off a rail or ledge a hundred feet and make the news.

"I hire from the orphanage all the time," Dexter said. "That's why when you said last week about callin' next of kin it was a laugh. Orphans work harder, 'preciate it more, show up every day and don't sass back. And lemme point out, when they hurt, they don't call momma. If they on your job, you they momma, and you treat each other right."

Dexter Philpot was not married, so it makes you wonder if he was good to them boys from the hungry father part of him, or if he was good to them from being a boy like them himself, only older.

It took a week to frame in the steeple and lay in decking, and another day to put up the new surface. The four of us worked

45

like the seven dwarfs, with an hour off here & there for afternoon storms. Sometimes we worked through the storm, though lightning was a scare. Oscar took a bad splinter in the side and had to go to Dr. Upperjoe to get it out and stitched up. He went by himself and was back on the job in an hour and a half, working his plywood to make up lost time, squinching his face and breathing shallow when he thought we weren't watching, for he took the pain back to the job with him.

Dexter treated us all to dinner at the diner that night since our part of the job was done. It was now up to the sheet copper man. He had two days to cover the steeple before Dexter's penalty clause kicked in and lost him money. The place was noisy with the tail-off crowd that comes in after the regulars, some tourists at the counter but mostly second shift fishermen and construction workers who use up the toothpicks and belch while saying <u>Uurp</u> your ass. A few of them said hello or so long to us, coming in or going out, for Dexter Philpot is well known in town and I am getting there. Everybody likes Dexter, not only because he is kind, like his daddy, but is also honest in business. Dexter told Oscar and Justin to get their own booth because teenagers think mealtime conversation means talking with your mouth full.

"Oscar hurtin'. Good thing the job is done," he said with his eye on the boy. I called the orphanage and told them to have they doctor check him out tonight."

I said, "You are a good man, Dexter."

But he was looking away with a big smile, and it was Grandy who answered it with her order pad and starchy apron. "Dexter <u>Phil</u>pot," she said, "Frankie told me all about your job he's on, didn't you, Frankie? Why haven't you been around to see me, you thoughtless boy? Didn't your daddy ever tell you, friends must tend one another?"

And they batted it back & forth a little while with Grandy telling Dexter all the bad news in today's paper until there came pauses and sighs and the smiles started to make their face stiff. Then we gave our orders and Grandy went over to take the same from Oscar and Justin.

I said, "You like young people so much, how come you never got married and have your own?"

"Because you got to fuss with women to do that."

"What's wrong with women?"

"Let me point out they's more women than men in the world, and anything they's more of is naturally weaker than whatever they's less of." Dexter took the salt & pepper shakers from their holder and made them twirl around each other on the table.

"First I heard of that," I said.

"It is only good sense. Take two batteries, for n'instance, one is old and one is new." He showed the pepper shaker is the old battery and the salt shaker is the new. "The old battery use up more of its power than the new and is weak. The new battery use up less of its power than the old and is strong. So anything they's more of is weaker than whatever they's less of." When he saw my face having trouble with the idea he said, "I'm not only a carpenter, I am part electrician too. I know about batteries."

I said, "Don't electricians fuss around with women?"

But he wasn't ready to give up and raised the salt & pepper shakers, "You dig what it is about the batteries, Frankie?"

"Yeah, yes," I bobbed my head, "I missed the connection is all."

Now he bobbed his head like he understood why I am dumb. "I know it is tricky; we can come back to that some other time. But just remember, women will mess you up. If you remember that, trouble will sli-i-de on by." He made a slide with the salt & pepper shakers back to their holder. "I know all about women. I could write a book. You ever do the camel?"

Grandy put our salads down before I could answer, then finger touched the orders on her tray. She called back to the pass-through, "Bishop, there's supposed to be two soups with this order. Get those soups up!" To us she said, "Sorry boys, start on your salad. I'll bring the soup in a minute," and was gone to her other tables. I saw Oscar and Justin eating soup and chewing bread and talking with their mouth full.

"I don't think I ever did the camel. What's the camel?" I said to Dexter.

"Hump, hump," he cupped his hands around his mouth and spoke softer. It sounded like he was in a bucket.

"Oh, right. I know what humping is, I just never heard it called the camel."

"See them fancy girls up at the counter? They's four of 'em, see? I never seen them before. Did you? No, you didn't, because they belong to that big Caddy out front with Illinois tags, bet five dollars on it. You didn't see the Caddy either, I bet. Maybe they tourists on the way to Miami Beach--"

"I did so see them. When we came in. I only didn't see the car or the tags."

Dexter said, "I am talking women, not cars. I say maybe they tourists on the way to Miami Beach lookin' for a good time with a stranger before they ready to go marry a broom and a mop. Maybe it's like they feelin' guilty for bein' rich and want to forget the foreign cars and big houses and massagers and tennis lessons. Or say they poor and one time even had a job-- say a typewriter in a office but the office went out of business. What will they do now? They will go to Miami Beach and marry some fool they meet tomorrow, or they will go to Miami Beach and do the camel wif a Cuban and then go back home and divorce a trustin' man. Rich or poor, they are losers. They will make losers out of men they put the finger on. They forget good things people done for them and only remember the bad done to. They forget the bad they done to others and only remember the good. It is a balance made in hell and they have brought hell to Locutan tonight right here in this diner. I would like to point out you cannot say the same thing about--"

I never heard the rest of Dexter's interesting talk because right then Grandy brought our soup, and the four girls paid up and left, gabbing and happy. When he dropped me off at Grandy's, he said, "Watch out for a woman that folds up her clothes and puts them away in a closet before she do the camel. That is poontang who got her<u>self</u> on her mind. She will bring you troublesome pain, troublesome pain."

Not before nor since have I seen Dexter's blood so riled.

*

The sheet copper man did not show the next day and no one knew where he was. Dexter came by and picked me up at Grandy's where I was thinking about putting in a new kitchen floor, and together we rode around, Dexter upset, and tried all the bars and liquor stores, for Ramon Taborda did like his grape. Later that afternoon, he called, sober, and said he was finishing a job in Naples but will be at the church 7 AM tomorrow, bring a helper for him-- two helpers is better-- and he will have it done by sundown. It was when we were eating a balony sandwich at Dexter's house that the phone rung and Dexter put the squeeze so hard on his roll, the insides zapped out and fell on his shoe.

So I called the orphanage whilst he cooled off and told the lady who answered to please save Oscar and Justin for Mr. Philpot tomorrow.

"Oscar and Justin must be in school tomorrow," the lady said, "and they are already saved."

"Who am I talking to, please?"

She said, "This is Sister Mary Margaret."

"Oh, well I understand what you are saying, Sister, but I have just spent the last two weeks on a job with Oscar and Justin for Mr. Philpot, and nobody said a word about school. Are we talking about the same Oscar and Justin?"

Now she said, "And who am I talking to, please?"

"This is Mr. Farley, assistant manager of Mr. Philpot speaking."

"Tomorrow is a school day, Mr. Farley. Oscar and Justin must be in school," she said and her voice was even and friendly.

"Excuse me, Sister, but what about the past two weeks?" I said.

"They were magic-word days, Mr. Farley."

"Magic-word days? I never heard of magic-word days."

"Mr. Philpot has," she said. "If he is available, I'd like to speak with him."

So I handed the phone to Dexter and he said Uh-huh a couple times, and then, "Sure, Sister, same as before." He put the telephone down and said to me with a smile, "She told you about magic-word days?"

"Yeah, she did."

"Five dollars each, That's the magic word."

The next morning was cool. A spanky breeze flapped the palms above three blue herons that were fishing a pond behind the church with one of them saying, "Wark! Wark!" Ramon Taborda's truck was there with a beautiful spool of copper sheet shining in the sun, four foot wide. He got out of the truck when he heard us pull in, and gave the once-over to Justin and Oscar when they jumped down off the bed. Oscar held his side after he jumped.

Ramon said, "What's wrong with him?"

"Splinter, stitched up. He's okay," said Dexter.

"Uh-uh, no way," Ramon shook his head, "I'm not payin' for him. I'll make do with this one," he pointed to Justin.

Dexter stepped in front of him, "Look, you already screwed me out of one day, and tomorrow I'm on a penalty with this job. If you don't finish up by tonight, I'll deduct yesterday's money from today's, and you'll go home with nothin'."

"Bullshit, I don't contract for time, I contract for job, and you damn well know it, Dexter. If I do this job in twenty fuckin' minutes, I get full pay."

"And if you're not done by tonight, I take out my penalty from your check. The whole thing."

Ramon thought for a minute, then shook his head again and said, "I don't need this bullshit. You can shove your steeple up your ass," and stomped to his truck and jumped in. After a few seconds where he rummaged in all his pockets, he yelled, "Who the fuck took my keys!"

I went over in front of his truck and jingled them at him, then tossed them to Dexter. He ducked them in a pocket. There was a stretch that everybody stood stiff, ready to see which way the minute would jump, and then Ramon began a little smile, then scrinched out a laugh, and Dexter said, "Haw," and slapped his leg, and I said Ha-Ha and the boys hee-hee, and before you know it, all of us laughing like fools at 7 AM. When we quietened down, we heard the heron say, "Wark! Wark!" and all bust out laughing again like it was a Bugs Bunny & Elmer Fud movie. Ramon said he would give Justin a day's pay if the other three of us did backup chores free, and Dexter said he would work free but would pay Oscar and me himself.

Ramon Taborda was the best sheet copper man I ever saw. He made the fit without a bubble and put a shining skin on that steeple with such perfect splicing, solder and rivets, you would think it was a thirty foot cone of fire in the sun. The four of us lifted, held, ran, carried and cleared for him. There was not a move he made nor a tool he needed that was not serviced on the spot or slapped in his palm like a TV doctor. We laughed from the bright beauty of it and couldn't take our eyes off. The higher he went, the more risky it was because he could not use a ladder track on the copper, which would mark it. Instead, he slung a rope around the lightning rod on top and hoisted himself with it, shoes off, spraddled like a frog. He worked his way around the steeple like that all morning and afternoon, no break for lunch, course after course. The sun was orange when he got ready for the last half-course, and now he hauled Justin up, shoes also off, to hold the cap in place while he put the rivets in and soldered. But Justin wobbled and dizzied up so high with no harness and nothing at his back to give the feel of safety.

Down below on the scaffold, Dexter watched every breath. "He's goin' to fall," he whispered. "You and Oscar space yourself around on the scaffold. I'll take the bare side."

The bare side was all the way across from the scaffold on the other side of the steeple with nothing to stand on but the ledge of the plate that circled around the bottom of the cone. When he got around there he was out of sight to me and Oscar.

"Hold still," we heard Ramon tell Justin, "the God damn torch won't light," but Justin was making baby sounds like Wah- - Wah-- Wahyah-wahwah! and his palms squeaked trying to hold tight to the copper sheet whilst he started slipping on the way down. His face was twitching and his eyes open wide. I was scared and holding my breath, not knowing which angle his fall would take, when all of a sudden his knees and palms could not keep him there another second and he fast took a half turn away from the scaffold, screaming and sliding down the steeple like a brick on ice. I screamed too, from the fright of it, and jumped off the scaffold onto the plate ledge, another fool without a harness, still too far from Justin's angle to do him any good. But Dexter Philpot was scooting around his little toehold towards me to make up the difference when Justin's feet hit the ledge throwing him back into space, his arms slung out wide like he would fly the rest of the way. Dexter and me each caught an arm and held tight, then wobbled from the force and weight of him. I gagged, with my face stuck flat to the copper sheet and my other hand squat-palmed against it. The ground was sixty feet below.

"Move!" Dexter yelled.

So we took little baby sliding steps and jiggled back to the scaffold with Justin hanging between us like wash, except he had pooped himself. He was hollering all the way, for he busted an ankle when he hit the ledge. Up top, Ramon Taborda hung with his mouth open. It was all so fast, he must've got caught between curses. Oscar gave us all a hand up onto the scaffold.

The finish of it was that Ramon paid Justin double wages and also the doctor bill for his busted ankle after he made him swear he would say the ankle got busted some other way, some other place and not whilst under the hire of himself. Dexter said it was a fair plum, and also wise to duck trouble from the state inspectors even when it seems far off. "I done it myself more than once," he said.

The next two days, people came by on foot, in cars and bicycles to see the new steeple. It was beautiful with the golden shine of new copper and there was a man from a magazine that took pictures. "This will make you-all famous," he said. On the third day we had a storm off the gulf that hit with hard winds and rain sharp as needles. Lightning hit the steeple rod twice which started a fire that simmered at first then exploded into a blaze that slammed and popped and seized anything of wood. A day and a half later, the whole church was char-- all but the new steeple, the copper skin now only a shell, a thirty foot black cone on its side on the ground. Somebody forgot to reclutch the lightning rod. It never got grounded. The lightning rod took the heat from the sky and never got grounded. I told that to Dexter. He wiped his face and took a deep breath.

He said, "I would like to point out how hard times comes in threes, Frankie. First, Justin nearly is killed and busts his foot, and second, this here--" he waved his hand around the black and smoky wreck-- "this here terrible thing."

I said, "You just said threes. That's only two, Dexter."

He said, "And the third is--" he took a paper out of his pocket. It was a paper with holes and many dots where letters used to be. It was that new computer paper, three colors of paper. He took another deep breath and tore it up into little pieces. It was the bill for his work.

Later, when we took a club sandwich at the diner, he said,

"What's a profit, Frankie, anyhow, when it gives people only more trouble on top of other trouble?"

4

HoHo Murn

"You've got the address and you know how to get there, right?" Taylor Binns said. "You'll pull into the muster yard."

"Yep," I told him. We finished off our coffee and went outside. It was a chirpy morning for the night's rain had washed out the air and the green was almost hard on your eyeballs. You could hear the harbor chop slapping against the sides of the boats a half mile away. "What is a mustard yard?"

He cast me a fearful look, as if not knowing about a mustard yard cancelled everything else I used to know. "Muster yard--m-u-s-t-e-r. The place used to be a soldier's barracks in the war. Appleton and Murren took over the buildings and made warehouses out of them. The muster yard is in the middle where all the buildings-- on three sides, that is, because the open side lets out to the roadway-- where all the buildings flank around it and the soldiers were called to fall in. Uh-- meet and gather, is what "fall in" means. They use it now for deliveries in and loads out. Got it?"

"I hear snook is runnin' on the out-tide," I said, after I told him yes I got it.

"No rush, it's early." Then he said like somebody left a pin in his shorts, "Oh! I almost forgot, Junior, I need your social security number," and he patted his pockets for a piece of paper, then whipped out his taxicab logbook to write on.

"Don't have one."

"Sure you have. Everybody has one."

"Never got it."

"Impossible. You're not anybody's dependent-- how d'you pay your income tax?"

"Don't pay income tax. I never really had an income-- only odd jobs."

"You need it for your benefits-- you know, like, well like food stamps or government assistance, or SSI." Mr. Binns was getting excited.

I shook my head and said, "Sorry, never had them things either."

"For Christ's sake, Junior, you-- you can't register to <u>vote</u> without a social security number."

I didn't want to answer him back on that one which was so logical if you been following the other answers. Instead I said, "I don't have fingerprints either."

Mr. Binns made a snort and tucked the taxicab logbook under an arm whilst he held out his palms to me. "Show me your hands."

"I don't mean I don't <u>have</u> fingerprints, I mean my fingerprints never been took by anybody. Nobody, never. When trouble comes, I always leave before it starts writing things down."

He put the logbook in his pocket, took a big sigh which became a yawn, and after he finished with it he pushed the baseball cap back on his head and said, "I'll have to pay you under the table."

"Neither did anybody ever take a picture of me," I said. "A good idea when you are on the road."

Then Taylor Binns said, real quiet, "Jesus, Junior, you're one lost lamb all right."

An hour later, after he and Esau got the pickup loaded, I was glad to see he became his old gabby self. First he gave me a pair of monster sunglasses and then he took off his baseball cap and stuck it on my head. "Today will be a blazer, you'll need these. Pull up your shirt collar when you're driving into the sun." Then he looked at his chickens in the crates which were hollering their head off and said, "If you want to raise chickens, Junior, you got your Americans, your Asias, Mediterraneans, English, Polish, Hamburgs, Continentals, Games, Orientals, Orna- mentals and Miscellaneous. You must calculate how active they are, do you want them for meat or eggs or exhibition or fighting. You got to think about size, proportion, plumage, skin, rate of development, do they fly or not, temperament, hardiness, are they fickle & fussy brooders, brains, disposition, will they lay at six months age or before, cost of production per dozen eggs or per pound, easy or hard to feed, will they forage & scratch with courage, egg quality, meat quality, mate easy or not, how many hens per cock-- should be one to 25 or 40-- molting quick & regular or not, and how responsive are the earlobes to change in color pigmentation." Taylor Binns took a deep inhale and got ready to go on, but I turned and made to hoist myself up into the pickup where twelve crates of chickens made more racket than a grammar school band. It didn't stop him. He said, "You'll be carryin' Wyandottes today, but we've also got Buckeyes, Javas and Plymouth Rocks. We were thinking of Rhode Island Reds, but--"

About the time he said the word <u>Reds</u>, I twisted the key and the pickup motor finally drowned him out. There is too much to know about chickens. When you are young, white meat or dark is enough.

*

"Mr. Murren no here," an old guy said without a shirt. "Murio el domingo pasado." He was brown as a coconut and a hairy Spanish accent. He stood in front of the truck, in the driveway of the delivery yard holding shut a gate right off a main street where cars were already backing up behind me with everybody's hand on the horn. "Siesta. Lunch. No os senteis. El pollo no!" he yelled.

Behind him in the yard a dozen men were laying in the shade. Two or three got up, not liking the horns. One young guy came to the gate and motioned me to drive up on the sidewalk so the traffic could pass whilst he then argued with the old man & finally slapped him on the head till he yowled and ran off. Then the new man opened the gate and let me in. I saw his pants had a nice crease and his shirt was clean.

I parked the chickens out of the sun which was a blazer, right next to a building where other crates of live chickens were stacked. It was so hot the sky looked yellow and everything made of wood-- empty chicken crates, painted signs, the stakes on a stake-body truck-- crackled & popped. A washed out sign was painted right on the brick wall of the building that said Appleton & Murren Import/Export Foods. Then I put on the monster sunglasses and tug the baseball hat peak way down to cut the glare and went over to thank the young guy who had laid down again. "What was the old geezer hollerin' about?" I said.

He opened his eyes and woke up enough to tell me, "He say Mr. Murren he die last Sunday and you and your chickens do not seat yourselves. He is called Don Antonio and wakes up only when others sleep. He is mad but low in wages."

"Mr. Murren died?"

"No, only the one who <u>call</u> himself Mr. Murren, he die. Don Antonio he mix up."

I said, "Do you whack him on the head every day like I just saw?" but before I could push my point, which he must of heard coming, he shut his eyes again, so I walked around the muster yard to three buildings trying to find an office until a man eating a peach in a blue plaid suit with a good haircut and a clipboard stepped out of a door in a shady wall and said, "You lost? You Taylor Binns's driver? That your pickup over there next to those crates of bird?" His voice was dry & tight around the peach chewing, like a fresh pretzel.

"Yes to all three. It's good to find somebody awake. Will you sign for mine and have your boys unload so's I can be on my way?"

He first looked down at his high-shine shoes, then up with a smile. "My name is Jonnybo-- with an $\underline{X}$. You must be new, right? A new man behind those glasses under that hat? The rule here at Appleton and Murren is, Mr. New Man, is you bring 'em, you unload 'em." He spit out the peach pit in his hand and flung it against the brick wall where it exploded and out flew the nut. A smart pigeon sailed off the roof and gobbled it followed by a bunch of dumber pigeons. This also showed me that a blue plaid suit and a haircut can fit a bird lover as well as a poor-spelling businessman with bad manners. There will never be an $\underline{X}$ in "Jonnybo."

"I am a driver, not a forklift, Mr. Jonnybo."

He shrugged and sucked his teeth, "Suit yourself. You'll find the road back less crowded than the road here, I hope."

"My job was to deliver the chickens and there they are." I thumbed at the truck.

"No, you delivered a truck with chickens on it; you have not delivered the chickens yet."

I saw I was stuck and could not argue a road around his idea, for there is a slippery way to talk if you are a businessman that uses regular words which do not add up to their meaning and also change meaning whenever you decide-- without telling anybody. In the middle of thinking, he stuck a business card in my face. I took it and it said Jean Jeanibeaux, Appleton and Murren Import/ Export Foods. Underneath, it called him Vice President.

I made a little whistle and said, "There is an X." Then, like it was hard to swallow something so grand, "You are vice president of chickens?"

It looked like he puffed out a little. "You could say that."

"Did the chickens get a vote?" I said, slipping the card in my shirt pocket.

*

I finally unloaded the crates myself for I am small but wiry. Once siesta was over, the gates opened and trucks rolled in like it was a signal. Nobody paid attention to me but ran around pulling things off one truck and loading them on another, the whole thing in Spanish. I stacked my crates next to the building where I had parked in the shade, on top of the crates already there. I made a check mark on mine with a hunk of chalk handed to me by Mrs. HoHo Murn. My chickens started clucking at the chickens underneath them which clucked back, and soon they was all so busy meeting and greeting and telling chicken stories back & forth with new friends that they forgot there was an axe waiting at the end of the conversation.

The reason I unloaded the crates myself is Mrs. HoHo Murn. She came out of the office looking for Mr. Jonnybo and stopped up short when she saw me arguing with him. I stopped too, and for all I know so did the pigeons flying in the sun. She was so strange and beautiful that it felt like I wanted to cry. I guessed thirty years old and small with a smooth forehead and dark hair flashing the light brighter than Mr. Jonnybo's shoes. Her long eyelashes hung under big lids-- remind you of beach umbrellas and the eyes were blue with real eyebrows, not paint. There was a giant bow in her hair which gave her the look of half girl, half big-head butterfly not human. Her lips were plump with a perfect round chin. When she came closer, I could see-- which started a motor in my stomach that was new to me-- I could see the dark hair in her armpits under a summer dress with no sleeves, and then came a breath of the musky smell on her that must of crossed my eyes for Mr. Jonnybo fuzzed up in the corner of my sight.

"You're from Locutan? Taylor Binns's delivery? I'm Josephine Baranski. Take this chalk and check your crates as you unload. You'll have to hurry because the gates are about to open and if you don't get out soon, the trucks will trap you in here till after closing. There's no back way out. When you're done, come into the office, sign the invoice and pick up your receipt. Hurry now." She put a big hunk of chalk in my hand and went back in the building with Mr. Jonnybo sniffing behind her where I wanted to be.

HoHo Murn is how the boys in the muster yard say her name. Her right name is Josephine and they mean to call her JoJo, no disrespect, but they can't say it right and it comes out HoHo. Also <u>Murren</u> in Spanish is <u>Murn</u> which is how they say it. All this I learnt waiting in line for my receipt. I did not learn why she calls herself Baranski.

It was dark when I got back to the farm with Esau and Mr. Binns there waiting for me. Mr. Binns was mad & crazy all at once with Esau talking at him like a kind man to a puppy and came at me after I parked and tried to hand over the monster sunglasses and baseball hat to him.

"What happened!" he hollered and moaned & groaned, slapping himself on the head with more moans & groans and did not take the glasses and hat.

I said, "I couldn't get out in time, I'm sorry. The muster yard got crowded and all choked up with trucks and me in a corner where I was stuck till closing time. No way out except the way in. I know it is late." He kept it up with a weep & wail like I did not give my explanation which was my reason and excuse and the truth also, though not the whole truth that I will tell the rest of right after this. I thought it was a mighty fuss Mr. Binns was suffering for a few hours late with everything else I had to do. "Mission accomplished," I said and held out the receipt. This started him to howl & yowl all over again.

Esau knew that I was in a fix and not understanding it. He stopped trying to cure Mr. Binns and came over to me with my mouth open and ready to jump clear soon as I got a hint which angle all this was coming in from. I been jammed before and know ways out.

"Mr. Jonnybo called up Mr. Binns," he said. "From the import-export. Bad news. The load all has to be killed."

I didn't catch on. "Killed? Sure, yeah they must be killed. Don't they have to be killed before they're et? I never seen anybody eat a live chicken."

Esau shook his head, stuck a finger in his ear and scratched an armpit. "No, you don't kill layers, you kill meat birds, and then only right before they are froze. Somebody stacked your crates right on top of a load of contaminated birds. If they're meat birds you can pluck and dress 'em right away and no harm done for the local market, but you can't market contaminated lay-ers, they must be gassed. Mr. Binns's Wyandottes, they was layers."

"What is 'contaminated'?" I said, a whisper, being a little nervous and shaky in the voice.

"Chicken fleas, chicken lice, chicken mites and chicken tick. They eat up the young birds and worry the layers so they stop layin'. They should of stacked your load way clear of that spot. If Mr. Binns can find the fool who done it, he might could get his money back after a time."

"What happened! How did it happen?" Mr. Binns yelled again and whacked himself on the ear.

Just then we heard the sound of a loud motor behind us and in a second the tow truck pulled up with Taylor Binn's brother-in-law Rudy driving and passengers Grandy Cumberhouse with Valerio who jumped out and started barking at Taylor Binns for the noise and upset he was making.

Grandy climbed down saying, "Thanks for the lift, Rudy--my stars, Taylor, what a racket you're making. Control yourself." She went up under his nose and said it two more times. Then she came over to me and said, "Rudy told me what happened at the dropoff. Are you all right? I made him wait while I called there after you, you were so late I got worried. When Taylor phoned to see if you'd come home instead of here, I imagined terrible calamities-- I've always said you are a responsible young man. You know how things are in the world, you know what the papers say every day-- trouble everywhere and people don't care about anything anymore. Nobody knows for sure how Taylor's birds got into the contaminated pile-- they say it's the worst infestation anyone's seen in years-- but he stands to lose the whole shipment unless he can prove it was their negligence. Did you see anything?"

Grandy was in a housecoat with slippers on and it was clear to me that the ex-mayor's phone call had woke her up. This was almost worse than anything else and began to upset my nature, which was dangerous for me since I saw trouble was about to climb up my back and a cool head is all that can keep me ahead of it. Whilst I pretended to try remembering if I saw anything, rolling my eyes up and holding a kiss-pucker on my lips, Valerio stood and put his paws on my chest with a big stretch. I held him and he licked my face with little love noises in his throat.

Then Grandy said, "Frankie, who is Greg Loomis?"

Taylor Binns was still complaining and moaning so loud that a couple bats made their jerky-fly overhead to see what was the racket with Rudy and Esau trying to ease him down. Grandy hopped over there to help and I didn't have to answer her question; but I knew someday soon, maybe tomorrow, I would. And just like that, Father, just like that, one thing and another, it looked like it was maybe getting time to leave Locutan.

5

Greg Loomis

What also made me late getting back to Taylor Binns's chicken farm, besides being blocked against the wall in Appleton & Murren's muster yard by big trucks, was waiting in line for my receipt from Mrs. Josephine Baranski. At least that was the first part of it-- waiting in line. But that only took a half hour or so; it was what happened afterwards that really kept me from leaving and made me late.

In the loud little office with a bare bulb and a few chairs and a fan turning in a corner, she sat alone at a desk full of nicks and scratches on top, checking off the slips handed to her by drivers and once in awhile telling Mr. Jonnybo who stood behind her to have somebody run outside and count up a load one more time. Everything she did was fast and decisions with no bother. She never smiled once and there was even a little frown if you got up close, which made me remember she had not smiled when we met earlier out on the platform either. I am talking about smiles from the heart, not smiles from the mind for I have come to understand that smiles from the mind are the same as no smiles at all, and they happen to people good in business-- like Josephine Baranski-- who are fast and decisions with no bother. People who smile from the heart end up poor with weak friends.

Flies were thick and quick. You could feel the heat from outside and hear the traffic rolling out the dust on the road. When it was my turn she looked up at me and told me to have a seat, there was a question or two. I picked a chair-- it turned out for the afternoon-- and fell asleep in the lull of it still with my dark glasses on and the baseball cap down on my nose, and next thing I knew a rap on the ankle woke me, the sky was orange and Josephine Baranski was biting me with words.

"Wake up, wake up. Where d'you think you are, hobo heaven?"

I rubbed my ankle. "Did you just kick me?"

"Take that stupid hat off, and those stupid glasses. Where are your manners? Stand up."

I got out of the chair and as I was waking up saw the door was closed and the windowshade down. From inside the big warehouse, I could hear work going on with machinery and box sounds and quacks and clucks. I said, "What else?"

She was not patient, and I figured wore out from a long day's work. "The hat I said, take it off. And the glasses. What is <u>wrong</u> with you, can't you handle more than one idea at a time?"

I took them off, sorry for her that she was riled over such a dumb thing. Then she stepped back and stared at me with her eyes and mouth opening a little. She could of been a bit wacko mixed nuts, so I said, "You told me to wait because there were questions. Then you asked about hobo heaven and you asked about what is wrong with me. I thought you meant chicken questions. I will answer only chicken questions and no questions about myself. Now I am ready to sign the invoice, ma'am. Can I have my receipt and go?"

She didn't hear me and got quiet and practically whispered, "I thought so," still squinnied at me. "Turn your head this way and that."

"My receipt, please, ma'am?"

"Turn your head; do it." After I did it, she said, "How old are you?"

I said, "If I leave right now, I still won't get back to Locutan until nine. They'll worry about me--"

"What's your name and how old are you?"

"Look, Mrs. Baranski, I'm on a license that I can't drive after dark--"

"It's already dark. What is your name?"

I took a deep breath. I been here before. "Greg Loomis."

"Greg Loomis, huh? Let me see your driver's license."

"It is in my other suit," I told her.

"Uh-huh, no license," she said. "Let's see your social security card, Greg Loomis."

I shook my head and gave her my helpless look. "Private stuff, ma'am. Personal stuff."

64

"No driver's license and no social security card? What happened? Lose them?"

I made a sigh and turned down my mouth, "I will have to leave without my receipt, is that it--"

"The first thing I said to myself when I saw you was, 'He is too clean for a chicken man'. Do you bathe every day, Greg Loomis?"

Though that is a question I don't mind answering, I said, "I'll let Mr. Binns call you and settle this, and I can swear he will be plenty mad when he gets to it. He is mighty fond of his chickens. You do not want to get him mad about his chickens. Please have somebody open up that gate for me."

"Would you like to know what the second thing I said to myself was?" She was close to me and I smelt that dusky smell that made me swallow two or three times. I would have to leave without what I came for. She said, "I said to myself, 'Everybody has a double'. Greg Loomis, you are, top to bottom and side to side, the image of someone I know. Have you ever been to a dentist? The person I'm talking of has never been to a dentist."

"Mrs. Baranski, I got to go. It's past my dinner time and I am bound to be late when I get back to Mr. Binns. Will you tell somebody to open up the gate?"

"You're not going anywhere till we've had a talk. A long talk. There's a Hamburger Jungle not far from here. If you don't mind hamburgers, I'll treat you to dinner. Don't turn me down. I think this may be important to your future."

Now Father, I know that all travels begin with the first step and mighty oaks grow from little acorns, and all the other sayings that warn us not to turn off the world when good times seem so far away. But there is also another side to the sayings, the side where bad times that drown you today once started from the littlest thing way back when. Like here in this case with Josephine Baranski, I am not turning off on the world nor even waiting for good times-- but if I would of turned off on that hamburger, all this trouble gets nicked in the bud. Who can tell me no to that?

We drove in her car, a BMW convertible, dark red or black, I couldn't tell at night. At Hamburger Jungle I had the Nile Special-- two Gorillaburgers and a Crocodile Coke. The burgers had three little pickle slices set on top to look like two monkey eyes & mouth. The French fries came in a piece of cardboard folded over to look like a tree, and the coke was in a mug with a crocodile shaped like the handle. The place was lit up, clean and shiny with smiling people behind the counter happy to serve. We got the last booth, for the place was full and noisy with a warm food smell. Mrs. Baranski stared at me the whole time and did not order anything for herself. Dusty Broom once told me when somebody watches you eat without also eating theirself, you are putting yourself on the losing side. He said you can not go one up whilst cud-chewing and your cheeks full of food with the other party sitting there pretty in a normal face. So I began talking to show her I am not impressed and also able to be a gentleman with interesting talk for dinner. "We passed two hamburger places on the way here, one also a Hamburger Jungle," I said. "Why is that?"

She said, quiet and staring, "They don't know me here." Then she said, "You look enough like my husband to be my husband."

I don't much care who I look like. "Mr. Baranski must be in bad shape," I said, going for a laugh.

She nabbed one of my French fries and stuck it in her mouth but did not lick her fingers, using a napkin instead. I admire good manners which Grandy Cumberhouse is always on the bandwagon of. "He has a mustache, though. Have you ever grown a mustache? His father died when he was very young and when his mother remarried, her new husband adopted him. He kept the Murren name on the business because it's been Murren and Appleton for sixty years. Everyone calls him Murren anyway."

The first Gorillaburger was delicious so I squeezed on ketchup and started the next without saying anything about names. Also the coffee smell was fresh and deep and I ordered one. I told her, "I never grew a mustache yet."

She said, "My grampop used to tell us kids about the grain harvests when he was young in Texas. It took eight weeks with three hundred hands working night and day. Thirty tractors pulled the reapers and two hundred migrants shocked the sheaves. There were twenty-one sheaves to a shock and every tenth shock was for the migrants. After the harvest, there was a four-day cookout with Spanish music, big kettles of chili and stew and barrels of red wine. Late at night the kids were put to bed so as not to see the lovemaking when the dancing ended. My grampop was twelve; he had an older sister, nineteen, and a younger, ten. They lived in the manor house like the old southern mansions, twelve columns and forty rooms. My great-grandfather was a doctor in Chicago and the farm was a getaway, a hobby you might say. His wife was a queen, my grampop said-- his mother-- past forty then and beautiful, always made up and in high heels-- Grampop said she needed two maids to dress her for dinner. Bed linen was changed every day."

I was getting full but went on biting and chewing since it looked like this would be a long story and no need for me to say a word, but I said to myself, I never had a sheet till I came to Grandy's house.

"At Christmastime, the servants-- there were twenty-six of them-- gave out cakes and cookies and candies they had made for weeks, baking and boiling syrup. The day before, two pigs were buried in the ground and baked in a fire for eight hours. They were served on Christmas Eve on real silver platters with all the servants at the table. At midnight they went to church in the sleighs with neighbors coming along, singing and ringing bells. The Mass was sung to Spanish music and hundreds of candles. On Christmas day at noon the feasting began again with games and dancing and visitors from all the little towns nearby. Grampop said that was 1938, because that year the three children got horses, beautiful horses trucked in from Kentucky.

"Then the war started in Europe and the military draft came here. Army bases were built everywhere, and airfields for Army Air Force training. The soldiers harvested the wheat and loaded it on trains for San Antonio. They took the tractors, then the cows and pigs and finally the kids' horses. Of course the family was paid for all of this, and my father told me it started the idea in his head of the import-export business, but it was still robbery, thievery. Union Confiscation, he called it."

I finished the last lump of burger and chomped the end of the fries. Then I used the toothpick that came with the meal, holding up a napkin in front of my mouth for manners. The place was still noisy which I didn't mind for it was mostly friendly hollering back & forth. It was people in between working or in between going home or killing time because nobody's there anyway.

Most dinners at hamburger places fit in one another of those slots.

Mrs. Baranski ran on with her story. I know her name is Mrs. Baranski but I thought of her as Murren and she is known by most as Murren, and what you are known by lasts a long time, whilst names can change. Look at me.

"Did I say my Grampop was an Appleton? Well, he was. And on the next farm were the Murrens. Get the picture? Grampop Appleton and Grampop Murren were not only neighbors, they were friends, and so were the families, and when they each had a son, the sons became friends. The Appleton son became my father and the Murren son became my husband's father."

"You married the neighbor's kid," I said.

For the first time I saw a little smile. "I'm glad you're paying attention, Greg. Yes, his name's Harry, the boy next door, but by that time, both families had lost their farms. Everything went-- the money, the servants, the great houses. It was price controls and shortages of farmhands and livestock after the war. That's when family farms started to die off, you know. Times were hard then, and we went from rich to poor-- well, <u>almost</u> poor. But my daddy remembered when <u>his</u> daddy was paid by the government for the grain and animals they took-- and would've been paid more if there'd been more to sell-- and he got together with Mr. Murren and found out how to bring things into the country that Americans wanted-- cheaper clothing and South American beef and out-of-season fruits and vegetables-- and how to send American things to countries that wanted them. Oranges and sugar and-- well, chickens. Now it's computer chips and blue jeans and tennis balls, and they're talking about surplus arms-- you know, grenades and mines."

"And chickens," I said.

She gave that little smile again, "And chickens. Still chickens. Always chickens. So Murren and Appleton settled on the gulf coast here before Truman got his second term--"

Although it was very interesting, I made up my mind to stand up and she stopped. "Thanks for the feed, ma'am, and I am sorry to short your story, but I got to go. Maybe on my next trip you can finish, if you still want to tell me. There's no way I can explain to Mr. Binns how late I--"

"Don't be rude," she said. "If you want to leave this place, we can sit in the car out on the parking lot. Like it or not, you're going to hear this story, the whole thing."

So we went to her car and she drove to a dark corner away from the others. I asked myself what I was doing there with a stranger listening to a story about baked pigs and servants and families on sleighs at Christmas. Then I answered myself, it is probably because there is something up my backbone and in my belly-- a chill, a thrill-- to hear from a real live person about things my whole life been without and would always be without. And there is the person also, a beautiful woman close enough to smell, who is making a mystery around me.

"My father died a few years ago; heart attack. And then two years later, Mr. Murren died suddenly and Mrs. Murren married Mr. Baranski who was the financial officer for the company. People said they'd been having an affair but no one had any proof of that. It was important because Mr. Murren's death was suspicious-- he was found hanging from a fifty-foot tree and there was no ladder anywhere around for him to get up there."

"What kind of tree?"

"Huh? What d'you mean?" says HoHo Murn.

"I know about trees. The right kind of tree, you can climb. Maybe he climbed it."

She turned those eyes on me and locked my tongue. "He only had one arm, Greg-- didn't I tell you that? He lost it when he was a boy, a farming accident. A thresher, I think. So the sheriff decided there's no way a one-armed man is going to climb that tree, much less do all the hanging work. He figured it was either murder or someone aided and abetted a suicide; a friendly act of love for a sweet man whose wife was two-timing him."

"So he went for the murder idea, huh?"

"No, there hadn't been any homicides in the county so far that year and he said this one wouldn't be the first. And he changed his mind about suicide-- it wouldn't do for a prominent family like the Murrens. He had the coroner call it accidental death, but people still think otherwise. And that's because Peter Paul Baranski was such a rotten bastard."

I said, "Peter Paul Baranski became your father-in-law."

"Yes, and took over the business and cheated customers and beat his new bride and son whenever things didn't go right anywhere in his life." Her voice was sharp and tight and it sounded like hate for him. "The beatings, they made my husband anti-social, an introvert-- you know what that is, Greg? It's a person who leaves the dark only when it's darker outside. For God's sake, almost no one besides office staff can say for sure what Harry looks like!"

"Get a lawyer," I told her. "Lawyers fix anything." Then I let out a yawn, but she didn't catch it.

She took a big breath and made her little smile again. "It won't be necessary. Baranski died last week. He was driving too fast on a back road and lost control of his car. He sailed over the berm and landed in a canal full of alligators. The sheriff said they found his jacket with his wallet in it."

I remembered the old man at the gate who said Mr. Murren died, and the young man who said No, it was the one who only called himself Mr. Murren. But all I said was, "The 'accidental-death' sheriff? He found the wallet?"

"The same," she said, "but this one is not accidental death quite yet. Soon, maybe. First they question suspects. They'll probably question my husband soon-- that's why he wasn't in the office today. He's taking a couple weeks off in Miami Beach to get his head together. They'll be questioning me too, I imagine.

<u>Then</u> it will be accidental death. Open your mouth and let me see your teeth."

"What?"

"Please, Greg, open your mouth." Then she brought up a flashlight and looked at my teeth, every one. "Have you ever been to a dentist?"

"What for?"

"I thought so. You can close your mouth now."

"Are they saying maybe your husband or you killed his father?" I thought, It is not possible for you. You would not have to kill for what you want. Stay close and breathe on somebody and he will do the killing for you.

She said, and her lip gave a curl, "Not really his father; his rotten bastard <u>adoptive</u> father. For control of the business, sole control. It's a very, very good business. I'm the last Appleton, my husband's the last Murren. We make good suspects."

"Not you," I said, feeling my eyes go soft. And then she leaned on me and kissed them, my eyes, one time on one and again on the other.

"Call me Josephine, Greg, and the last name's Baranski. Pretty, huh? Promise me you'll come back," she said, "and I'll tell you about your future. Take this; keep it and think of me. It's the sash to my mother's wedding dress-- very dear to me." She untied the ribbon from her hair and stuffed it in my hand. "Promise me you'll come."

I promised, and she took me back to Mr. Binns's pickup where I got on the road which took awhile to stop shaking. All the way south I smelt her hair ribbon. A million bullfrogs sung like sticks rapping along a picket fence the whole way home. Dusty Broom once told me frogs sing for love when the season is right.

(I know I have said Dusty Broom told me this and Dusty Broom told me that, when the truth is, although he did tell me half the stuff I know, he didn't tell me half the stuff I give him the credit of. It is honest sayings about life's tricks I picked up in a million odd jobs from drivers and gang bosses and roadies like myself but cannot remember who said what. The reason I say Dusty Broom told me is people want to nail down their facts so they can feel sure about what they're hearing. Lots of times people say, "Who told you that?" or "Where did you get that one?"

If you say you picked it up someplace sometime but you just can't remember who and where, they will wave their hand and say Pish-Tosh or You don't know shit. Ever since I began to say Dusty Broom told me, nobody said that.)

I already told how I got home late and what happened there.

6

The Bishop of Locutan

This is the part where I meet you, Father, although you know we sort of met a couple times before.

The next day after Josephine Baranski kissed my eyes, I finished up my chores at Grandy's house and then hopped over to Esau's to feed what was left of Mr. Binns's chickens. Rain started, warm and soil-smelling, then quit and started and quit again. I learnt by now it is the way rain does here in deep Florida. Then the sun came out & dried everything up, like the world is wash on a line.

When I started to ask Esau about women and what it means getting your eyes kissed, he said to go see the bishop. He wasn't mad and he didn't let on that he just naturally knew it was my fault about the chickens and the fleas, ticks and mites. I think he wanted me off the place before Mr. Binns showed up. Grandy told me Mr. Binns was going out to the import-export himself to get the birds after they were gassed and bring them back to bury them, which a man from the state said he must. A rented backhoe and operator would do the funeral.

I asked Esau where to find the bishop and he said, "Either at the printer's, the diner, or here. He ain't here, so he's at the printer's or the diner."

When I tried the diner first and asked is the bishop here, they told me he was on the late shift today, try the printer's. The printer's is across the street on a cattycorner, the cashier pointed. Can't miss it, it is also the town newspaper office, the monsignor works there.

At the newspaper office there was a man in an inky apron hurrying back & forth to a press that was clanking and banging, a girl with ink all over her hands watching the man run back & forth and also you, a tall, clean man with a good haircut and one gold earring. I knew right away you were Bishop, the short-order cook at the diner, also the man I saw digging with a shovel one day at the chicken farm. You were holding a box of shiny paper strips with no printing on them and looked like you were waiting to get at the press.

Father, I wrote down what you said and what I said that day, so I am saying it straight now. It was you that told me to write things down worth remembering, which I have been doing. When you noticed me at the printer's, you said, "I'm next."

"Okay," I yelled over the clanking, "but you should straighten people out that your name is Bishop and not the bishop."

You laughed and handed your box of papers to the inky girl. You yelled, "Elsie, make sure Horace sets this up when he's finished the run. I'll be over by the library." Then you motioned me out with your head and when we got outside you stuck your hand at me and we shook.

"I'm Chuck Allensworth," you said. "I'm the bishop of Locutan. Let's go sit in the shade. At least there's a breeze today. Your name is-- ?"

I told you I was Frankie Farley and you said Over there, the bench outside the library. "Well, what was the library," you said. "It burned down two years ago and there's no money to rebuild."

"This town sure needs help," I said.

You said, "It does." Then you said, "How old are you, Mr. Farley?"

It was the first time anybody called me Mister, and I must say there is a feeling in the shoulders that lifts your head and puts an inch on your chest. But I didn't let on about that because I had to ask about women and kissing on the eyes. Also there was a chance you had to be twenty-one to talk to a bishop, like drinking & voting. So I said, "Twenty-one."

"Twenty-one?" he said, spreading his eyes like a saucer and eyebrows raised up. "I'd have sworn you were ten years older."

All my life I been taken for younger than my real age, now here I am being taken for older. In my insides I felt it was something Josephine must've put on me, like a spell. And I have to tell you, Father, from that day on, nobody ever took me for younger again.

"Did I hear you're living at the YMCA down in Naples?"

"No sir, I don't know where you could of heard that. I stay at Grandy Cumberhouse's."

"Grandy's? That's good," you gave your head a nod, "that's good. Mostly, guys live at the Y so they can meet themselves under another name."

You were not talking the way I expected a bishop to talk. "What kind of bishop are you? Where's your uniform," I said.

Then you gave me a long onceover with no answer and we sat down on the bench. An animal said, "Urk, urk, urk!" close enough to make me jump.

"The canal is right back there," you jerked a thumb over your shoulder. "Nobody tends to it. That could be a seal for all we know, or an alligator."

"Once in awhile I think about alligators," I said to let you know I was listening. "But the reason I want to talk to you is this person--"

"I've made a little study of alligators," you said. "It's not true that they avoid humans-- I should say where they're not often disturbed or interfered with by humans. Those that have had dealings with humans do tend to shy away. But the others, they are ferocious and persistent, and big. A full-grown male is fifteen to twenty feet long, can you imagine? Not long ago, one of them came out and carried off the town donkey."

"The town donkey? This place has a town donkey?"

You said, "It used to, but no more," and really sounded sorry. "When the female gators are in season, the males roar so loudly it sometimes sounds like thunder. Do you know why they have such a disagreeable, unpleasant smell? It's because of the two ducts under their throat. They pour out a strong musky fluid. They have frequent, terrible battles over the females. You can't imagine their strength."

I noticed before that some people in Locutan like to explain things they are interested in even if they are talking to a watermelon. I figured you were on your way to a sleeper like the one Taylor Binns did to me on chickens, so I tried to spike your tree. "Yes!" I yelled, "That's it. Alligators are strong."

It made you jump and pull your eyebrows back down. "Very strong," you said. Then you turned away and waved your hand, "No one tends these gardens either," and I saw we were in the middle of a shady spot with long grass and weeds but also white, pink and purple flowers when the breeze pushed the grass apart. The flowers looked just like little bells. "Grandy Cumberhouse told me about Mr. Binns's chickens. Are you in trouble? Did you want to see me about it? Is there something you need to tell me?"

"No. But I reckon bad news travels fast."

You bobbed your head Yes. "I got a call last night to see if I could come over to do something to help Mr. Binns. He was taking it very hard. When I got there, that's when Grandy told me."

"Were you able to help him?" I was sad for Mr. Binns but scared for myself.

"He's agreed to work within adversity. The birds will be destroyed and he'll bury them himself on the farm. Taylor Binns is a solid man and one of the hardest workers I've ever met."

I checked your eyes to see if I could catch a smile but they were empty. I said, "I have not seen a single Catholic church here. Are you a bishop of someplace else?"

"No. I'm the bishop of Locutan, like I said, and my church is wherever I happen to be."

Some boys, maybe six or seven hookey players, kicked a can down the middle of the street then ran and elbowed and kneed each other on the way to kick it again. The littlest kid was always the loser but did not cry. He picked up a stick and evened the score on a couple bullies. Two trucks turned the corner where you & me were sitting and squashed the can flat. The boys grummeled up the street, raising dust.

"You're in a ripped Miami Dolphins tee shirt. You wear an earring and your blue jeans are tied up by a rope. You say your name is Chuck. I don't mean nothing smart-alec, but what kind of a bishop is that?"

You gave me a grin and said, "Fifty-five and home at last. I see no one's told you my story. I guess that means they've finally accepted me."

I been thinking lately, people want to tell me stories.

"I don't mind saying it, Frankie-- everyone else knows. I was fired from my diocese, a half million good Catholics, a fair-sized city just a bit off Lake Huron. Michigan. I wasn't happy with policy on the poor and homeless, and I probably had too much to say defending homosexuality and supporting marriage for priests. There were other matters that involved individual choice rather than religious doctrine, in my opinion. Then there's my daughter, too. I got on television, I was in the papers--"

I said, "You have a daughter? Are bishops allowed to have kids, Catholic bishops?"

"No, not strictly speaking, but my daughter was born before I became a priest. You saw her over there at the print shop-- Elsie, covered with ink. It's a sticky issue with them, the hierarchy-- I told you, individual choice rather than religious doctrine. They showed me the highway."

I didn't know what <u>hierarchy</u> was, so I said, "I don't get it. How can you fire a priest?"

"Yes, it's permitted. They can remove you-- the system, who knows, anyone from locals to the National Conference of Catholic Bishops to the Holy Father. But bishops are ordained by God, you know, and can't be taken off the rolls unless they're excommunicated. They must have a diocese-- it's called a titular see in my case and others like it. So they'll find one in a place that doesn't exist anymore like abandoned cities and areas that once were busy and full of people but got swallowed up, and ghost towns and struggling poor places. Yes I know, it sounds a lot like Locutan, doesn't it?"

"But you're a short-order cook, and they said at the diner you also have a job at the printer's, and I saw you myself digging a ditch at Esau's place. If you're a monsignor, why are you doing buck-a-day work?" I heard a cat's meow in my voice. It is a sign I am getting tense.

You hunched your shoulders and half closed your eyes with a fake grin. I saw the eyes were blue and your hair spotty gray in the shade. "Body and soul keeping together. Paying the rent, though it's not much more than a one room shack for my daughter and me. Eating every day. The bishop business doesn't pay much, Frankie, when the goats and chickens outnumber your parishioners, and <u>monsignor</u> is a secular title. Dorcas made clothing for the poor--"

I was trying to figure a way to remember <u>secular</u> so I could look it up later when a bunch of ladies came walking past. They all had dresses with some kind of flowers on it and fanned their-self with hands and rolled up newspaper. They were very old in their sixties. Every one said Hello Bishop or Good day Bishop or How're you getting on Bishop. You said something nice with each lady's name in it. When they were far enough down the street, you said, "They're on their way to bingo. Half the ladies in town show up every day after lunch, God bless 'em. The old feed store down there with the big front window, they cleaned it out and painted. Now it's a kind of civic center. We're full of old empty stores here. Not only empty stores either; there's a brand new warehouse complex on the other side of town that was built and then abandoned when the tenants went belly up before they ever moved in. Two buildings, one forty thousand square feet and the other, ninety thousand. This is a hard luck town, all right, and it's a crying shame." Then you looked at your watch and stood up. "I have to get back to the shop, Frankie. Horace is probably finished running my work off and it all has to be boxed and sent off this afternoon. They're bumper stickers and gags. I do gags-- did I mention that? Also I'm trying to organize the Catholic Horse Breeders of America--"

"But I need to talk to you, Father. It's really important."

You checked your watch again, "Talk to me on the way," and we started to walk back.

I talked fast and hit the high points about Josephine Baran-ski and the story she just <u>had</u> to tell me, but I did not say her name, and how her confidence in me gave me feelings she started which I knew the reason of but not the meaning for, and kissing on the eyes.

By the time I finished, we were back at the printer's and you jumped in with me behind to get your work. You opened a box and pulled out a strip with fancy blue lettering and stretched it between both hands. You said, "This is for Palm Beach and the rich bitch trade." On the bumper sticker was <u>IUD BY GUCCI</u>.

78

Then you said, "This one is for bakery trucks." It said <u>HANDS OFF MY BUNS</u>. Then another with smaller printing: <u>I'm such a loser. I came in third in my own lookalike contest</u>. "Gags," you said. "You can condense your life into gags."

All I could think of was I just gave my secrets to a bishop who has a daughter and says <u>rich bitch</u>. I started to go but you put a hand on my shoulder and said, "A kiss on the eyes is symbolic, Frankie. It's meant to blind you to illicit love." Then you scratched your head and said, "On the other hand, you might pray the prayer of St. Augustine. <u>Lord give me chastity, but don't give it yet</u>."

Dusty Broom once told me love makes hunger and hunger makes squinty-crosseye where you cannot see the trouble you are already in. Then he said there's a laugh at the end of your life, and it is on you.

7

Beautiful Ostrich

Linoleum cannot be laid below grade or on a concrete slab, so I had to use vinyl in the kitchen, more expensive and griping Grandy who finished reading the morning's bad news around the world to me about the same time I finished the floor. She was in a grouch mood because she has been sick with the cold she caught at Dr. Upperjoe's office that was getting worse and no sign of getting better, making her weak. She already missed three days of work and today had to take her breakfast in the living room with her bathrobe because of the floor job. When she got on to local news it perked my ear up. Her voice was small and a worry to me.

"Here's one, Frankie. Remember, from the other day? Accident Questioned. The accidental drowning death of Peter Paul Baranski, 64, prominent local merchant, is getting a second look. Baranski's car has been under examination by a team at the Ft. Myers forensic mechanics lab. Sgt. Chip Tomczak, assistant head of the lab said, 'The disk brake calipers appear to have been tampered with.' The condition of the brakes is all the more curious considering that Baranski's car had recently undergone a complete brake overhaul."

I said, "Go back to bed, Grandy, I'll hang around here today. Rudy can take the truck up for Mr. Binns. It's only crates anyway he's getting rid of."

"Baranski's car had recently undergone a complete brake overhaul, did you hear that, Frankie? Overhaul, my foot-- shoddiness and greed is what--" She started to cough & hack and I helped her to her bed.

Later in the afternoon, Taylor Binns showed up, and you, Father, you too and your daughter Elsie, to give her a cheer. But she slept through the three of you. We all sat and talked about her, and Valerio stopped by everbody's foot for a whinny and a pat on the head. Then when you were about getting ready to leave, Esau came around with a nice bass, all cleaned and boned

which he baked in the oven with carrots for Grandy. You &
Esau hung back and nibbled at it for Grandy was weaker than
before and couldn't eat. Esau helped me lift the furniture up into
the kitchen now that the new floor had set. Everybody said what
a good job of it I made with the corners fit and the cove tight.
Then two bingo ladies rung the bell carrying rice pudding and
custard pie and came in to gab with the bishop, but as soon as
they got a look at Grandy they whispered Get the ambulance.

At the hospital in Ft. Myers, she had pneumonia. Taylor
Binns followed the ambulance in his cab with Esau and you in
front, Father, with Elsie on your lap, and me and the two bingo
ladies in back. There wasn't much talking except for one lady
who had a little mustache and a man's voice saying, "Taylor, if
you ask me, now's a good time for you to set the date. It is just
the thing to give poor Grandy a boost," and the other lady that
looked like a pretty bird said, "That's right, Taylor. It'd chirk
her right up for you to surprise her and set the date." You and
Esau sort of bobbed your head.

Now I was not born yesterday, and I understood what those
ladies were getting at, but in all the time I been with Grandy
Cumberhouse and ex-mayor Binns both separate and together, I
never heard a sweet word from either for the other nor a 'dear' or
'honey' between them nor seen them squeeze a hand or stop for
a hug. That is why set the date run a rasper up my gullet: it
meant either I been left out of things complete & all together, or
I been so smothered in my own sorry life that I never took notice
of theirs. Both ways, I am low in the ratings.

I saw Grandy and Mr. Binns like a couple ostriches who
could not find love with other birds. Ostriches better think each
other is beautiful or it is the end of ostriches.

In the hospital we all sat down in a room where the TV was
on baseball and nobody watching. Esau turned it off and then
we just sat for a long time. Elsie was friendly and came over in a
corner with me where I was sitting and asked if I believed God
would help Grandy. She has a strong face with eyes wide apart
and a straight bridge to her nose and looks right at you. Then a
nurse peeped in and said the patient is resting comfortably and
there is nothing more you can do here, why don't you all go

home and get some rest, tomorrow is another day. We rode back in the cab with everyone talking hope. I kept my mouth shut, but before we all went our way, I told Elsie, "I don't mind if God helps her, but I would like to do something myself."

The next two days I cleaned up Grandy's place, in corners with the scrubber and over the walls with the drymop, windows and bathroom scrub brushed and shining, carpets with the sweeper and cushions beat. The second day, Elsie Allensworth showed up to help. (Father, I know you know your daughter's name is <u>Allensworth,</u> but somebody else might read this and not know, so I must spell it out.) She is a big help and doesn't talk too much but only asks questions about life on the road. It rained now mostly every afternoon for an hour or so which cleared the road dust off the roof and outside walls. The grass got green and flowers fresh. Then, on the third day I took my hourly out of the tea can, up to date, walked Valerio over to Esau's who said he would like it just fine to look after a good friend for Miss Grandy and also mow the lawn as needed. We jawed for twenty minutes or so about fishing and chickens and alligators till Mr. Binns drove in with my wages and an extra twenty on top, a bonus for good intentions and not cheating on hours. He said he will wait till cooler weather and then fumigate the grounds before loading in a new batch of chicks, for you cannot have an egg without you first have a chicken.

This sounded like the beginning of an old and hopeless riddle so I did not offer my opinion but held out the keys to Grandy's place and said, "Please squeeze her hand for me and give her a hug if you are allowed that close. I will try to stay in some kind of touch."

That day showed me how to be sad. Not sorry-- because I been sorry plenty of times-- but sad. Except for that one time so long ago with Tiny Bascom that lasted only a few months, this was the nearest I have got to friends, and almost a family with even a dog. It made me miss Ralph.

But my heart was boiled and my insides fried. Sleep was like drip off a dishrag and meals tasted like my tongue was wrung out. Nothing told me to stay away from Josephine Baranski; everything told me to go to her.

I had a suitcase now which made it easier to thumb up to Ft. Myers. Drivers will sooner give you a lift with a suitcase than without, for it makes you look solid, like you have been some-place awhile and are on your way to another where you plan to stay; and if I could, I would.

When my last ride dropped me on a curb just outside the city, I found a phone and called Appleton & Murren. A girl ans-wered and I lowered the voice in my throat and said, "This is Mr. Taylor Binns, ex-mayor of Locutan and soon to start up a very big chicken operation. Please put on Mrs. Josephine Baranski."

In a snap a man got on and it was Mr. Jonnybo. "Mr. Binns, hello, Jonnybo here. I hope you got your birds in the ground okay. I can't tell you how sorry we are about your loss, but we've checked all the handlers and they're no help at all. The state inspector is satisfied that your shipment didn't carry any new bugs and he's willing to close the book on it. We hope this won't affect your dealings with Appleton and Murren because we do value--"

"Let me talk to Josephine Baranski."

Mr. Jonnybo was a little suprised and turned up the squeak in his voice, "What? Why, look here Mr. Binns, you're not thinking of going any further with this, are you? I assure you, there was no negligence on our--"

"If you don't put her on, I will next call my lawyer," I said with the lowest angle in my throat. The phone clunked down on something and in a minute Josephine came on, peeved.

"Mister Binns, this is Jo Baranski. I thought we had--"

"This here is Greg," I said in a hurry. "Greg Loomis from last week."

There was only a second slipped by, then she said something to Mr. Jonnybo sounded like Go down and flay the smotch, with another second to wait before she got back on to me. "Greg? Where've you _been_? I expected you to call days ago. Where're you calling from? I-- I thought you changed your mind. You did promise to come back, you know. D'you still have my bow? Greg, are you there?"

The sound of her choked me. Also that there was a push in the back of it calling for me; me and nobody else. "I'm on the road here, south outside town. Can I come see you someplace?"

"I've already made the arrangements. Do you have any money?"

I said, "About fifty bucks."

"Good, good. Get a cab and go to the Citrus Queen Motel. The Citrus Queen. It's on Hibiscus somewhere near Magnolia-- the driver will find it. Did you get that, the Citrus Queen Motel?"

"I got it."

"Good. Go to the office and pick up the key for room 29. I left a little note for you, make sure you ask for it."

"What kind of note?" I said.

Her voice got quiet on its edge, "Personal, Greg, a personal note. You'll see." Then she got back to business, "Now, the reservation's made but you'll have to pay for it. Just ask for the key and sign in any name but your own. You know that, don't you-- any name but your own? Don't talk to anyone, don't get friendly with anyone and talk. Just go right to room 29 and wait there till I call you. Room 29," she said like an army drill.

"I need to eat first, grab a sandwich or something. I missed breakfast and lunch both," I said.

She said, "Aaah," in the sorry way people mean Oh you poor dear. "Of course, of course, though I'd like it better if you stayed out of sight. Well, there's a fast food real close to the motel-- you can't miss it, but don't get in a conversation with anyone there either, all right? It's what-- around three o'clock now? Three-fifteen, yes. Okay, I'll give you a couple hours to eat and clean up and I'll come by for you at, say five-thirty. Is that all right? Five-thirty? Be ready to go when I get there; don't unpack and don't leave anything behind."

Her voice was smoky. I said all right and she hung up. She was coming by for me.

Once when I was little, Ralph handed me a present for Christmas that he made me put under the tree and swear not to open it till morning. The house smelt of pork roast and spruce. Glass balls with snowflakes jinkled when you went past the tree and tinsel sparked your eye so that sometimes you had to duck your head away from it. The last thing I saw that night in bed was my present under the tree that I carried in my head until sleep came.

The first sign of light let me sneak out of bed pretending it was morning enough to be awake. I opened Ralph's present a little and peeped inside and smelt it, then a little more and touched it with my finger, then a little more and it slid right out in my hand, not my fault. It was a rowboat made of a million toothpicks, a perfect rowboat a foot long with little seats and even oarlocks. Painted gray to the waterline, then red around the keel. I made a picture in my head under the tree lights wearing Mama's old bathrobe of Ralph working on it every night after I went to bed, night after night gluing toothpicks while the city smogged and rainstorms banged the windows and trucks outside rummeled the glasses in our cupboard. Mama saying Go to bed Ralphie and then making tea for him.

When Mama went to bed, Ralph cleaned up after himself, folding up the broken toothpicks and scraps and ends in the paper he worked on top of, careful with the glue that took the finish off furniture if you were not gentle with it. Ralph in my head, in the forests we learnt to hide, in the snow under mountains where frost fuzzed our axeheads and our own sweat would freeze the shirt on our back, and in the tents for cards & smoking at night with the owls crying after voles. Ralph telling me not to be scared of the giant trees we could hear creaking a mile away at the cutting stand where the generators run all night to keep the heat on motors in the freeze. The trees, iced clear through and finally cracking like rifleshot, one or two tumbling slow, carrying others with them and crashing earth with a bounce or two, blowing up eighty-foot snowbombs in the dark. Animals chittered & ran off.

I have been hanging onto Ralph because I need him, no other reason, though the memories run like rats sometimes, too slick to grab. But I think I must let go of him if Josephine Baranski is in my future, for my heart can only hold one idea at a time. It worries me to think this way, to say it out loud, and I'm afraid maybe it means I'm putting my brother on the cheap; but, Father, she is coming to pick me up.

The Citrus Queen Motel was in an old grove that gave way over the years to roads and gas stations, but orange trees still cozied it and kept it quiet in the shade. The trees were full of green oranges that sagged the branches and brushed high grass on two sides and in back of the place. Out front there was fresh slag on a big driveway apron off the smoggy road and concrete behind which laid clear back to a walkway in front of the rooms. Healthy Royal palms flanked the concrete parking lot and two big rigs and a pickup sat in their own slots. With a service station on the corner and a fast food joint next to it, you could think you were in any town in any state in the USA.

I decided to check in first for a washup and then eat afterward. In the office was a tall pink boy sitting in a chair in front of a little counter with a pigtail in a black tank top. His hair was orange, shaved in steps up to the noggin where a clean ribbon of scalp laid front to back and two tiny rings lit his nose. He was listening to a song on the radio with his eyes closed and smiled when he heard the door open.

"Hello, I am here for room 29," I said.

He said, "Twenty-nine? Cool," and got out of his chair in time with the beat of the music, bobbing his head, flicking his elbows and slapping his knees all the way around to the back of the counter. When he opened his eyes I could see his pepper-flake pupils. Stoned. He clicked off the radio and said, "You can sign in right here. It'll be $36.95 one night including tax, phone calls extra. Ice in the breezeway next to washern dryer."

"You have a note for me-- room 29, right?" I said.

"After you sign in, man."

I set my suitcase down and pulled the money out of my pocket. A couple bills and some change fell on the floor along with some string and paper clips and a beat up card that when I picked everything up turned out to be the card of Mr. Jean Jeanibeaux, vice-president of chickens at Appleton and Murren Import-Export from the day he handed it to me there. "Sign in where?"

"Huh?"

"Sign in where? Where should I sign in?" I said.

"On the card. Didn't I give you a sign-in card?"

"No."

"Bummer," he giggled and bent down to get one which he laid on the counter with a ballpoint. "There you go, man. Sign in."

I copied off the business card and wrote Jonnybo's name, also the address and phone number on it. Then the pink boy handed me an envelope before I had a chance to ask for it again. I took the key and high-stepped down the walk to room 29, the first motel room I ever was on the inside of, if you don't count laundry rooms; I have snuck into motel laundry rooms on cold nights when I was on the road. Then I ripped open the envelope and it was a note that said, "Like I told you, we have a future, Yours, Josephine." There was $200 in tens, folded.

In room 29 I found a shower with a tub, so I took a bath with the shower on. There was a clock radio and TV too which I watched some beach volleyball on while the clock radio played. I hung up my jacket in a closet with Josephine's bow in the pocket and also put her note in there with it. The $200 I stowed in my pants pocket. Then I tried the mirror. I have not bothered much with my reflection since age eight or nine when I learnt that whatever trouble you're in shows up there. After Ralph died, I pretty much stayed away from mirrors.

I found out the pictures on the wall were screwed tight to it and a quarter made the bed shimmy. Then I put on clean under-wear, a clean shirt and socks and my jacket and hiked to the fast-food place out behind the gas station where I took seafood chowder, a turkey club with fries and ice tea, all paid with my own money.

She came early in the red BMW and gave me signs that she was glad to see me, all smiles but wearing a navy blue bandana on her hair with dark glasses. When I jumped in the car, she said, "Put your luggage in the back seat. That's it. I'm so happy you're a man of your word, Greggy," and gave me a peck on the nose. "You came back to me."

"Greggy?" I said, but I was thinking <u>luggage</u>, I have <u>luggage</u>.

"Fwum now on you'll be my widdle Gweggy, aw wight? Okay?" and she eased the car off the slag apron into traffic with a little girl pucker on her mouth. I never saw anything so beautiful.

"Thank you for the $200, Josephine. I will pay you back, don't worry."

She grinned wide, "Pay me back? Don't be silly, you'll earn every cent of it. The future, remember?"

"I'm nuts about you," I said, "but I got to tell you, I been bad luck to everybody up close. Things happen to people around me."

She thought for a minute, then said, "Me too."

"I-- I even talked to a bishop a few days ago, and although he did not give me the mumbo or jumbo of it nor I'm not saying I believe in the mumbo or jumbo, but for the trouble I made in my life if there is a soul and there is a hell, I am afraid there is a chance my soul will burn in hell."

"Uh-huh," she said, "then we will meet again, Greggy."

Nobody said much for a few minutes. At traffic lights she reached over and squeezed my hand once or twice and more than ever, I wanted her to hold a good opinion of me. "I signed in a fake name at the motel," I said, wanting her to ask what name so I could tell her the joke of it-- Jonnybo's name. But she didn't ask, and after a minute it didn't seem so funny anymore so I kept my mouth shut.

Finally she pulled into a mall center with a thousand cars in the lot and people coming in & out with packages and kids. "D'you have a wallet, Greg?" she said, and right away found a parking space up close to an entrance. She took off the navy blue bandana and shook out her hair. I saw earrings that looked like diamonds.

"Yeah, but it's really ratty. You don't want to see my wallet."

"I don't. I just want to know if you have any credit cards?"

"No, never did."

"Well, we're going into the mall to get you a new wallet and while we're at it, open up some charge accounts for you. What d'you think of that?"

I blubbered my lips, like "Ppfaw, nobody will give me a charge account. I never stood in one place long enough."

But she was geared up and didn't bother with my answer. "And then we'll go to the library and get you a library card. You'll have to read one or two books about economics and the import-export business-- you can read, can't you?"

It was a question, not an insult, and if I am heading for the import-export business-- which is the meaning I got from her words-- it was a question she should have the answer of. "I read the dictionary. I am careful about spelling and always look up the hard words. You will find that words I look up are spelled right, but I don't look up easy words so sometimes I get crossed up on them. That is the truth of my reading."

She said, "A man who tells the truth is rare, and I'm lucky to find you. A man's word must be trusted, Greg. Always tell me the truth." She got up under my eyes and blinked her lashes and I smelt the dusky on her.

"I will, I will. I promise."

"Okay. Now there's a branch library right across the street -- over there, see? Beside that lit-up building, the senior center and the police station-- that's the lit-up building. Next thing, you will open a bank account with your two hundred dollars-- the bank is in the mall with evening hours-- and after that we'll take a ride to a place I want you to see. How's that sound?"

It sounded like business was on her mind, which I told her. Then she took me inside to four famous department stores where I filled out credit forms for each one, with an address she told me to write down and also my employer: Appleton and Murren Import-Export. I had a job and never knew it! It pays to be friends with the boss. I got my new wallet in the first store, soft leather with little gold corners. All four places handed me a card with "Temporary" on the front and said feel free to use it up to $250, except one, the most famous of all, which said five hundred and after we verify you, the sky's the limit.

Josephine was happy and excited with color in her cheeks. She hung around perfume and jewelry counters while I was busy with the credit forms and later said that was because she wanted to show her confidence in me that I could take care of business with no help needed. Confidence in me, she said, which puffed my chest a little. And it was the same at the bank and the library, a savings account and free books with no help needed, but when I started to look around for a dictionary, she hopped off the bench she was sitting on and yanked my sleeve whilst holding her watch up for me to see.

"We're running late here, Greg. I'm sorry to drag you off, but we've got to go. You can come back another time for the books." We were in the library and she whispered it. I thought, Where you are says how loud you can be. I never thought of that before. Schools, churches, logging camps, football games. I would whisper for her and I would yell, if she wanted. I would clamp my mouth and never talk again. I would sing underwater for her.

When we got back in the car she said, "Buckle up, we'll be going past the Everglades." Then she made a pain face and yanked off her earrings, and then a laugh at my gasp which before I knew it, slipped out. "My ears aren't pierced, Silly, these are clamp-ons and they're killing me. Did you think my ears were pierced? Do me a favor and hold them for me, will you? I don't have any pockets in this outfit."

I stuck them in my jacket where I felt her bow and her note. It made me smile.

"Whatever you do, don't let me forget them. They're heir-looms." Then she paid attention to her driving which got faster and faster, swinging off the street and onto a two-lane road soon under banyan trees, the only light in the world coming from her headlights. Frogs were loud, louder than the car. Josephine sung little tunes now & then I never heard before, with interesting words. After she finished the first chorus, practicing mostly under her breath, she hollered, "Now everybody!" and wagged me a downbeat with her finger.

> "Limestone, potholes, lakes and streams,
> Sawgrass, springs and summer dreams.
> Scrub willow, wild myrtle, oak and bay,
> Custard apples, nod and sway.
> Papaya, cuke, and lemon tree,

Prickly ash and pine live free.
Deer, ibis and crocodile
Hope you stop and stay awhile.
Mighty heron, sweet egret
Began here, and they live here yet.
Beware-- behind each rubber plant
The gator does what the otter can't."

Then she yelled, "Everglades, Everglades forever!" and took her eyes off the road to see what I thought of her song. All around us was trees and water and peeping, grummeling things. "Well?" she said, not wanting to wait while I am noticing the speedometer is saying <u>65</u>. "I made it up myself."

"It is a catchy song," I swallowed, "but I personally don't care for the alligator part."

She squeaked and almost sung again, "Oh Greg, I'm so happy."

We passed through a two minute Florida rain that the wipers couldn't keep up with. I saw the green light from the dashboard hit her smile and make her look like a laughing ghost. I said, "Me too, I am happy," and thought maybe the two of us, Josephine and me, maybe we were ostriches who found each other like Grandy Cumberhouse and Taylor Binns. Ostriches-- me the ugly, her the sweet.

8

Greg Loomis Is Dead

In 1937, after years of dredges and clamshell ditchers-- also dipper and suction types-- and floating dynamite camps, the Everglades Drainage District opened the Cross-Florida Waterway, from the Atlantic to the Gulf of Mexico. It channeled 140 miles from Stuart on the east to Punta Rasa on the west. Punta Rasa is south of Fort Myers and north of Locutan. That is the history Josephine told me zooming through the Everglades when she took me to her new house that night, to show me around my future, she said. "All of Florida is on top of a limestone mountain."

She pulled into a drive and stopped under some trees.

"Where are we?" I said.

"Punta Rasa; our new place. Haven't even fully moved in, really. It's a brand new house, we haven't even met our neighbors yet." There was half a hazy moon and humidity dripped off the ends of leaves. "I know this must be terribly confusing to you, Greg. I promise I'll explain everything later. You get out here and I'll park the car. Don't get lost now."

A dozen steps out from the trees the place was lit up like an oil refinery, shrubs and vines and flowers on bushes crowding up to the house. I could see a wide lawn with a pond and chairs & tables around it. Hoot owls said <u>oogoo, oogoo</u>, and crickets clicked and said <u>chirt-chirt, chirt-chirt</u>. Up a long stairway of stone steps to the front door I heard wind chimes ringing. Then Josephine limped out of the shadow lugging a big bundle in the weak moon. I hurried over and grabbed it off her.

She said, "No problem, my fault. I should've asked you to come with me to get it from the garage. Carry it on up here to the front." She looked around the lawn and gave a little shiver. "Everything looks so scary."

"Only shadows," I said. Then I thought, 'I can make her feel safe. I <u>must</u> make her feel safe.' I walked behind her. "Is Harry here?"

93

She turned quick and said, "What about Harry?"

"Where is he? Is he here?"

"No, no he isn't. My husband is in Miami-- I thought I told you that. Didn't I?"

"Yeah, you did. I figured he might be back by now."

"No. Here, you go first-- up the steps there. Careful with that package."

I climbed the long stairs, balancing the bundle. When we were standing on the stoop and she stuck her key in the door, I said, "What is this here I'm carrying, Josephine?"

She said, "Clothes," and stepped into the house with me behind. "Just put them over there by the stairs. You can take them up in a minute. Would you like a drink?"

I dropped the bundle where she pointed and said, "Yes, I'd like a martini. I never had a martini."

She said, "Oh Greg, you do raise my spirits," and before I knew it, had her arms around me with an honest kiss for the real purpose of kisses. Then pulled me to the bar where she clattered up a few drinks. It didn't take long for everything to feel like cotton and standing on sponge; I am not used to alcohol. She kissed me some more and took my hands and put them on her body.

"Relax, Greggy, I won't break. Touch me here, squeeze me here."

I must've been happy sometime or other in my life, but it was all a mountain climb to get up here to this. I heard my voice, weak, "I am not so good at squeezing."

Then she showed me how to squeeze, and in a minute she said, "I think you're ready. Get the package and come upstairs."

She took off her clothes in her bedroom and said Do the same. Everything she took off got hung on a hanger or put in a drawer; I tried to remember, but couldn't, what Dexter Philpot said about women who put their clothes away before they do the camel. Poontang, he called them. He said, "Never forget what I'm telling you," but I forgot anyway.

Up in the bedroom, she showed me how to do things like I only saw dogs do before today. She made me put on a mailman's cap. "Take a deep breath," she said, "and let me have it." In a minute or two she said, "Oh, oh my God, deliver the mail, baby, deliver the f-fucking mail!"

*

In the morning, I woke up alone. Fresh flowers filled the room with beautiful perfume, and birds flew against the windows, tweeting and singing. There was clinking in the bathroom and pearly sunshine lit up pictures on the wall. I gave a big long stretch full of yawns and tried to hold my eyes open, but they kept shutting. Later, when the sun hit my face and I smelt coffee, I pushed up out of bed and put on a robe that was laying across the foot of it. It was soft and white with the initials <u>HB</u>. One wall of the bedroom was glass, and outside was palm and oak and deep, dark green things growing with sun shining in & out. It was a cool room full up with colors.

Downstairs in the kitchen when Josephine saw me she laughed a light laugh and skipped over and pressed up against me for a kiss. She was wearing a bathrobe too. "And how is my mailman this morning?" she said. She danced away back to the stove where bacon was frying and pancakes blipping on a griddle.

"I'm good, very good," I told her. "Uhh, I can't find my clothes. Did you put them away?" I tried not to yawn, but lost.

She smiled, though it was not a smile for joy. It had sly in it. "You won't need them anymore; you'll be wearing different clothes. As of today, you will live in this house with me and be called Harry Baranski. We will fuck morning, noon and night."

Now, Father, I have been around too many champion raggers to fall for one like this. I said, "Harry Baranski? Uh-huh, please make sure I get his checkbook."

"You're already in his robe. Actually, <u>your</u> robe, Harry."

"Where are my clothes?"

"Greg Loomis is dead."

I gave her a snurl look-- eyebrows up, mouth turned down. I said, "Jacket and pants, a nice shirt, white socks and black wingtips. My clothes. Greg Loomis's clothes. Josephine, tell me where my clothes are at?"

"Upstairs in your closet, Harry."

I was hungry and could not figure her game. It will shake out soon enough whenever she is ready for the next act. "Would you hand over a plate, please?"

"Only if you will be Harry Baranski--"

"I need the explanation first."

"You are my love, Harry," she said, and stroked a finger down my cheek, "everyday and undying. I promise. Greg Loomis is dead, drowned in the Everglades last night and taken by alligators sometime this morning, I would guess. He stole my car and had an accident. I couldn't sleep and called it in to the sheriff's office soon as I woke up. They'll find the car sooner or later, darling."

"After breakfast, I must get back to Locutan," I said.

That made her gulp down the mouthful of hot coffee she had swigged. Then she said, "Trust me, it would be a dumb thing to do right at this time. You'll see what I mean-- everything will be clear before you go to sleep tonight. Besides, in Locutan you are still Frankie Farley. You used up your time there, don't you think? How long do you want to be a gofer for losers?"

For the first time I felt an insult to myself when my friends were insulted. It says you have bad judgment. I got up and filled my breakfast plate at the stove.

She set a napkin at my place and went on, "Also, we have done a search on Greg Loomis and Frank Farley. We hired a computer service, a specialist, a tracer. There is no record of your life anywhere before Locutan. We did find out you've been telling people about time you spent in the northwest. Logging, you said, and there's no record of that either. We're satisfied it's a dead end, and we're happy with that because the younger a person can be traced, the nearer somebody can get to who it really is."

"Why?" I forked in two hunks of pancake and a slice of crisp bacon, all with syrup, and swallowed the wonder of it.

Josephine put on a tender look, like somebody watching her puppy eat. "Because if we can do it, it means someone else can too. And when the police find my car in the swamp and what's left of Greg Loomis, we want that to be the end of it. Then you and I can love each other for always-- Mr. and Mrs. Harry Baranski."

"Who wants to know all this about me?" I said, noticing that <u>Mr. and Mrs. Harry Baranski</u> did not raise my breathing even a little.

"We do. The business. The office." Josephine wagged her hand like people who know their words are not clearing up the story by themselves.

"Tell your tracer to look up Anton Korsakow. My brother Ralph, his name was Franz," I said. "It is best to be sure." I knew this truth would jolt her at first, and then she would take it for a lie. Shock is medicine for worry because it makes everything else smaller, but people don't like that medicine and find ways to soften it up and get things back to their right size. Pretending the truth is a lie softens up shock. Besides, Anton Korsakow is the same as Andy Korso, Frankie Farley and Greg Loomis, isn't he? He is only a name, and names are finished when you stop using them. Yet all four names are in love with Josephine Baranski, I thought.

"You're some kidder," she said and whacked my head with her dishtowel.

"You killed your husband and dressed him up in my clothes, is that it?" I said it like the day's weather, no feeling one way or the other. What will fools do for love? I am one and I am here, is the answer.

She poured another coffee for me and flipped her tongue in a way that I knew breakfast would be over soon. "Harry was very sick, Greggy. He was making bad business decisions."

I said, "Look, no foolin' now, where's your husband, Josephine?"

"He will never vote another proxy, dearest."

My mouth dried up. "Where is he?"

"I told you, he is you, my darling. And you guessed right-- your clothes are in the Everglades. Your jacket and pants and shirt and white socks and black wingtips. They are on the man who stole my car."

"Your husband stole your car?" I sounded like a kitty mewing.

"Greg Loomis stole my car. They'd find him in it if they only knew where to look, though, like I said before, he may be at lunch with the alligators about now."

"The new wallet?"

"Also. With the new credit cards and passbook and library card."

Then she must've got tired of my questions for she dropped her robe and was naked, except she held out the mailman's cap in one hand. She said, "Mail call."

*

"Don't you want to know about saprophytes and epiphytes and parasites?"

"No."

She punched up the pillow behind her head and got under the mussed sheet. "But you have to. And there are other Harry things you should know about."

"You told me he stayed away from people. You said people hardly knew what he looked like. But soon they will get to know me and know what I look like. Who will care about peppiphytes and all that?" I made a big yawn but covered it for the sake of manners, and that made me wonder if manners count anymore when you know you are taking a dead man's place.

And like she read my mind, she said, "If the two of you stood in different rooms, people would say it's the same man in both places."

The sun had gone above the trees and left her bedroom in deep green shadow. Now the furniture had a shine that lit dark corners off its reflection. The flowers smelt sweet and birds flicked & peeped outside the windows. On her back in bed, her beauty made me a dumb ox. I looked sidewise at her perfect face. I will pull your wagon till I fall, I said to myself. Somebody told me that horses will work till they fall. Was it Dusty Broom who told me that? Tiny Bascom? Later on, Josephine rose up on an elbow, "Listen, I hear a car coming. Yes, yes, it's turning into the drive-- d'you hear it? Get up, get dressed, my darling. Hurry."

She was up and into a pretty housecoat before I was able to cough and say <u>What?</u> I remember how once I had noticed the way she made decisions. A swipe in front of the mirror and a finger-tip of lipstick, and here was Josephine Murren Baranski running downstairs, ready for the doorbell. I fell back down and, later, once heard a snore. Who's that? I said, Who snored? I think I dreamt of Grandy Cumberhouse, but I am not certain. Grandy snored.

"Harry Baranski. Harry Baranski!" a man's voice, all business, woke me. I remembered voices like that-- the sound of somebody who knows he's got the edge. "Wake up, sir, wake up."

I opened my eyes and saw uniforms, though the bedroom was now in the afternoon dark. The first thing I noticed was the flowers smelt sweeter, but I could not hear birds.

"Get up, please, you'll have to put on your clothes and come with us, sir." It was a man in a sport jacket and slacks who talked, and the <u>sir</u> was sarcastic.

I said, "What?"

"Harry Baranski, you are under arrest. Do you understand what I'm saying? Get up and put your clothes on right now, sir."

Then rough hands grabbed me and stood me up and wouldn't wait till I snuffled my nose clear or yawned, but hustled me to a wall and made me wait while they tumbled Josephine's bed apart and looked in the closets. After awhile, the man in slacks said, "Do you want to call your lawyer, sir?"

I blew my nose and frowned and looked at him and said, "What is it, please? I'm arrested?"

He didn't answer but sent out the officers who had grabbed me, then waited while I got dressed. I put on a shirt which I found in a dresser, and a striped suit, the shirt whiter than Grandy Cumberhouse's dishtowel, then the socks and shoes which were a bit loose, and a tie. In the mirror, I was surprised to see I looked like a businessman.

"I am Peter O'Malley from the sheriff's office," he said.
"I'm a county detective. You are under arrest for the murder of Peter Paul Baranski."

My stomach always tells me the truth. Here is a nightmare beginning. Before I could say anything else, Josephine showed up at the bedroom door with a deputy behind her. "Oh, you poor dear," she said, and tried to run at me, but the deputy nabbed her. She sucked into his arms and sobbed. Only I could hear it was too splashy, a fake sob.

"I don't know any Peter Paul Baranski," I said. "Josephine, tell him."

But she was still sobbing and leaning on the deputy.

The detective looked like he had heard all the stories of the world and mine was a poor one. "I must read you your rights." And he did, though I didn't hear a word.

They fingerprinted me and put me in the county jail saying Mr. Baranski this and Mr. Baranski that, like it was a hotel and Mr. Baranski was getting a good rate. I waited for Josephine to come in and put things straight, but she didn't come and didn't call.

Later that night, a lawyer did show up who said, "Mr. Baranski, my name is Thigpen, Marshall Thigpen. I am proud to represent you in this case, sir. You are the highest profile defendant our office has represented in a criminal matter since Senator Tom Thomas, back in '69. Of course, our corporate division has been doing Appleton and Murren's work for years."

I told him I was not who he thought I was and I needed clean underwear.

"I'll see to it," he said. "You are in serious trouble, sir, very serious trouble. Homicide is not with which to be trifled. Do you remember Senator Tom Thomas, Mr. Baranski?"

I did not remember Senator Tom Thomas and told him the same. I said, "Why aren't you asking me about the stolen car which was reported this morning instead of Senator Tom Thomas? There is a body in it. My body."

He tilted his head down and looked at me over his specs with one eyebrow hiked up. "Your body?" Then he riffled through his notebooks, two minutes of it, once in awhile looking back up at me whilst I was hoping to hear from Josephine any minute now. Finally he said, "It is my job to keep you from the rope,

100

sir. Aha-- I have the record of your wife's call to the police right here. The car was stolen-- uh, less than 24 hours ago. Do I have it right?" He wagged a paper in the air without looking at me. "The car has not been found, Mr. Baranski-- and please do not mention bodies to anyone, for we must fry one elephant at a time, sir, though Senator Tom Thomas did occasionally drive recklessly through Tallahassee on his way to legislative chambers. Before the charges, of course. You remember Senator Tom Thomas? Fraudulent use of public funds?"

"I never heard of Senator Tom Thomas."

He ignored what I said and spent the next hour trying to get my "version of the event" so he could map his strategy. He said words like <u>diminished capacity</u> and <u>self defense</u> and <u>extenuating circumstances</u>. Also <u>Everglades</u> and <u>ecosystem</u> and <u>plenty of water in Peter Paul's lungs</u>. But there was nothing I could tell him except I am not Harry Baranski, and he said that part would be the diminished capacity part if we needed it. "Mrs. Baranski tells me also you spent the past two weeks in Miami Beach to get away from pressure you were under. If you were under pressure, that could work for us too. We'll call the hotel people when the time comes. You'll be arraigned in the morning and home with your lovely wife by noon."

The next morning Detective Peter O'Malley sat in my cell and laughed when I told him about this conversation. "Thigpen goes a long way with his Mr. Fuddle act. Don't underestimate him, he's got lots of surprises in that briefcase. And he's right, we haven't found Mrs. Baranski's car yet, Harry, there's only your old dad with no prints, in his own car in the canal-- but you know that, of course. There's not a whole lot to go on. The epitheleal layer is missing, but the alligators left enough for us to identify, like business papers and such. Also there's his dental records. Now Thigpen tells me you're talking about another victim somewhere in your wife's car? Please, how would you know that?"

He waited for an answer to this impossible question and the more I worked it over, the scareder I got. Why did my lawyer tell the police about another victim when he warned me not to mention it? The truth did not have a chance. As far as they could see it, how would I know about a body in the stolen car unless I was part of it all?

He said, "I see Thigpen's told you to keep quiet unless he's with you. Good advice. I just wanted to mention our forensic garage says your father's transmission was rigged and the brake lines cut through, all of them, every one. And you already know we have the tools you used to do the job. That's a puzzle too, Harry-- your wife let us search your basement without a warrant. Why d'you suppose she did that?"

I am accused of the murder of Peter Paul Baranski while the murder of Peter Paul's son in Josephine's stolen BMW is not discovered yet. When it is discovered, with a body dressed up in my wingtips, the complication of it makes my brain weak.

"Listen," I said, "one more time. I am not Harry Baranski. The point is, I am anybody but Harry Baranski is all that matters. You should be paying attention to who I am not. Harry Baranski is who I am not. Mrs. Baranski can give you the truth of it, and I don't know anything about searching the basement without a warrant. We are in love. She does not love her husband." Though I want to, I cannot tell him to go look for my new charge cards and bank book and library card which will be found under water someday, for how am I supposed to know about that? "You took my fingerprints-- check ours together."

"That's a weak angle, son, and you'd do better to drop it. You are Harry Baranski, and there is no record of your fingerprints anywhere. Until now, that is. I take it you've never worked for a city, county or state, and you've never been in our armed forces, am I right?"

"I haven't, but Harry Baranski might of."

"No, the FBI came up empty. They have no file on you. No Harry Baranski file. Of course, the prints we took from you will now identify you forever."

"Lord, what a mess I'm in."

"Pray, son," he said. Peter O'Malley was a nice fellow, mid-size, dough-faced and soft all over. Today he wore a tattered suit made of covert cloth from WWII and talked Tennessee in a syrup & baritone drawl, smiley, sort of friendly but without a point to his conversation. Not like movie detectives that know the answers before they ask their questions. His voice sounded deep inside him, like somebody was calling in a tub somewhere down his throat. Detective O'Malley said, "You've given me something to think about, Harry, but I been meaning to ask you, how's come you are not broken up over your daddy's passing?"

"I must talk to my lawyer before I swear to it," I said. Please call him, if it is not too much trouble."

Peter O'Malley bobbed his head and made a sigh. "Thigpen will be here for the arraignment in an hour. Can it wait till then?"

I will tell the lawyer the truth about Josephine if she does not show up soon on my side. "It can wait," I said.

Father, if you are wondering why I don't tell them my real name, it is because no name I ever had is real, and there is more trouble for me in the search of it, and trouble for friends I made along the way. When the truth sounds like a lie, everybody in it gets painted.

Detective Peter O'Malley told me stories about himself, but I was too much in the know to give him the same, his purpose. It is the purpose of policemen to make you give whilst you think you are receiving.

Waiting for Mr. Thigpen to show up, he said, "I knew your daddy."

"No, somebody else's, maybe."

"I mean your real daddy-- Mr. Murren-- who started your fortune. We were almost friends. I remember when he died in that tree and then Mr. Baranski married your mom. There was a lot of newspaper articles about it, like how did a one-armed man climb that tree?"

"I never met him."

"Your daddy went fishing a lot-- did you know that? We met on a party boat. He used to go out on party boats and not tell people his real name-- did you know that? Mr. Murren was a nice & friendly man, and though I was still very young myself, he confided in me, Harry. He said he liked party boats because strangers treated him same as everybody else even though he only had one arm. But he could bait a hook and cast and reel in with the best of them. It's practice, don't you think, and also playing the hand you got dealt."

"I am not Harry Baranski, Detective O'Malley." The sun hit the far wall in a slanty square. It had shadow jailbars in it.

"Then when I grew up and got into law enforcement, we met again. The sheriff sent me out to check on a story that your daddy was arming his people on the farm so they could shoot out tires on the pickups those produce bootleggers used to steal his crops. It stopped them, let me tell you. Well, you had three mules on the farm in those days that kept getting sick and the vet said it was the arsenic in the peach pits they ate. I don't mean they ate peach pits-- they ate the peaches that dropped during harvest when they hauled the wagons through the orchard. Your daddy was fit to be tied, Harry, he was so downright fond of those mules-- you know he was the last one in the county to go to tractors-- so he changed vets, and the new vet said no it ain't the peach pits, it's the elves. What elves, says your daddy, about ready to go back to the peach pit vet. It ain't your friends, says the vet, it ain't your family, and it ain't your enemies because your enemies are afraid to go near your place with that your men carry guns. So it must be the elves. The way to fix your mules is to find the one who is poisoning them."

This was a good story and almost made me forget my own raw deal for a minute. "He should have got rid of the mules," I said, "then he has no more mule trouble, and the same time, he crosses up the poisoner."

"Aha," says Peter O'Malley, "you think like a businessman, Harry-- you eliminate problems. That's good for a businessman but not for a detective. A detective isn't paid to eliminate problems; he is paid to solve them. See, even if your daddy got rid of the mules, I would still have to continue on and find who poisoned them."

"Why? There would be no more mules."

"True, the mules would be gone, but the crime would still be there. It's the crime that counts. Keep it in mind, Harry-- people on the street can forget and forgive a crime after awhile, but the law can't. It can't forget or forgive a crime that is not solved.

That's why the criminal receives a sentence; a sentence needs a period at the end. The law needs that closure. It's the system."

"I see why taxes go up," I told him.

The detective walked back & forth. It is a walk I have seen when people are working their way into an idea. "You know who poisoned those mules? I'll tell you who. Peter Paul Baranski poisoned those mules. Peter Paul Baranski, the same skunk who hung your daddy from that tree, Harry. But I couldn't prove the mule poisoning and I couldn't prove the hanging, yet here I am, proving somebody killed <u>him</u>. It is called irony, cheap and plenty of it in life." Peter O'Malley smacked his lips and shook his head like he had a taste of spoilt meat.

I said, "I heard it was the sheriff wouldn't let anybody get proof of the hanging. I heard he didn't want a murder on his books that year."

"Spilt milk," said the detective with a hand wave, like he was scrubbing my words off the air. "The whole point of my story, Harry, is I can see why you'd want to feed him to the gators, a rotten bastard like him."

"Never met him," I said, "and I am not Harry Baranski."

"Yes you are. Your prints are now in Washington in your official FBI file." He didn't say anything more but was looking up at my window where the sky had rolled in dark over the sun. Then rain fell and soon the jail was full of water sounds. There was dripping and sloshing, gushing and flushing, spilling and swirling, drizzle and mizzle, squirting and spouting, rippling and splashing, burbling and showering and sprinkling. Dusty Broom once told me birds stop singing in a storm and he was right. All I could hear was thunder cracking far away over the Everglades and once in awhile Detective O'Malley breathing, for he had too much weight on him, and the way he was sitting, it griped him in his chest.

"Someday I'm going to give this up and go find a nice job in security work. A lot of old cops are doing it," he almost whispered, like to himself.

9

If You Say Please, You Don't Have To Say Thank You

I don't hold it against him that Peter O'Malley is doing his tricks on me-- it is only what he learnt in detective school and would lose him the use of them if he didn't practice. But they are dull tools on me; I am an alien dropped out of the sky just three days ago that landed on love, and like Dusty Broom told me, love makes hunger, and hunger makes squinty-crosseye where you cannot see the trouble you are already in. Three days ago, I was in Locutan, in prime clear woods with my only worry being Grandy Cumberhouse sick in the hospital. Now three days later, I have a new wardrobe, I have a new house, I am married, I am in jail for murder, and my wife will not come to me. In the movies, there is music to tell you how to feel when trouble grabs somebody's walnuts, but there is no music outside the movie. I could use some music here.

Lawyer Thigpen showed up on time and led the parade-- me and two guards-- upstairs to the courtroom. There were three other lawyers already waiting with their own cases, and after a time listening, I reckoned they were a purse snatch, a shoplift and a break-and-enter. I was a murder-one, and being Harry Baranski besides, made sense of the people crowded up to the windows and doors outside.

"They are sure making a racket," I said after we took a seat at a table up front next to the nickel-and-dimers.

The lawyer opened his briefcase and started riffling. "It's because you're a celebrity. You put a spark on their tinder."

"It must be very dry tinder to get fired up on the wrong man."

He said, "To them, you are the right man, Harry. They won't like it if you take that away from them. Remember, public opin- ion is a powerful thing, and juries are made up of the public."

The little courtroom had a high coffered ceiling, hanging fans and schoolhouse light globes. The walls were polished chestnut paneling and the floor, a creaky oak. Up ahead of us was the judge's desk, big as a two-ton stakebody, fluted, beveled and curlycued by a smart hand. In fact, all the woodwork was smart quality, and it put me off Marshall Thigpen's words about juries and public opinion. By the time I was ready to tell him public opinion never stretched an innocent man's neck, the doors opened and there was a rhino stampede for seats that two scrawny bailiffs could not slow. The place filled up fast and set a buzz like yellowjackets in a tree stump. In a minute, somebody said, <u>All rise</u>, and we did as a heavy scowling man stomped to the desk wearing thick glasses. <u>St. Patrick Broiles presiding</u>.

"Watch out for this judge, Harry," lawyer Thigpen whispered, "he is a redistributionist."

"A what?"

"If he thinks you are guilty, he will want to stretch your neck. See, he hates rich folks, thinks they're all crooks and worse. Wants to do something about it. He hates them for his own sake, believes they think they've lent him his life."

"Then I am safe. I have sixty-three dollars total."

Marshall Thigpen said, "Ss-ss-ss," which was a laugh through the teeth, "He doesn't care what's in your envelope downstairs, he cares what's in your bank. He is a three <u>R</u> judge."

"What is a three <u>R</u> judge?"

"Repressive, righteous and reproachful."

The petty crooks all said they were someplace else when they got caught, not guilty. The judge said to talk it over with the prosecutor and come to an agreement before lunch because that will leave still time enough for a nice day, but if they go past lunch then woe on them, for there is no purse snatch, shoplift or break-and-enter alive that hurts as much as they will hurt.

"Isn't he something, Harry?" lawyer Thigpen giggled. "I admire him <u>so</u> much."

While I was worrying which side my lawyer is on, somebody called, "Harry Baranski, the charge is homicide in the first degree," and the audience started a rolling sound when they caught sight of me standing up. But before Marshall Thigpen could let out the big breath he took for talking, a uniformed cop rumbled in through a side door and handed a paper to one of the bailiffs who ran it up to the judge. Then the judge motioned for lawyer Thigpen and the prosecutor to come forward and they spent five minutes frowning, scratching heads and waving hands. St. Patrick Broiles frowned deeper, scratched harder and waved higher than the lawyers, for he was the judge and had a right to.

Marshall Thigpen came back to the table with his finger across his lips for <u>not now, be quiet</u>, and in a minute a bailiff squawked, "These proceedings is adjourned." Then when the crowd let loose a hiss and a boo, he said, "Stay calm, do not get unruly."

The audience didn't like it and stomped and whistled like a soccer crowd when St. Patrick Broiles hurried off his desk and disappeared, and before my guards could get me out through the thick of it, extra police rushed in to make them ruly. One woman got close to me and said, "God bless you, Harry, your family has gave my family jobs for sixty years," and a young man about my age said, "Fry, Fucker."

*

Back in my cell, Lawyer Thigpen explained what happened was, the note handed to St. Patrick Broiles came from the county prosecutor himself and said that Josephine Baranski's stolen car has been recovered from the swamp with a body in it with a number of questions that may cast doubt upon the charges against Harry Baranski, so they are being called back pending further investigation. "With one thing and another, they can keep you here two or three days longer," my lawyer said. "If the murder charge slips-- and it does look like it isn't holding-- they will have to find something else or let you go."

"I told you about the body; I told Detective O'Malley too. Nobody believed me. It's Harry Baranski in that car."

He stretched his jaw and showed his teeth, looking around with his hand up, signing for quiet. "No, it is someone else. They know who it is but they're not telling right now. And at this point I would advise you to stop saying you're not Harry Baranski. If I'm right, it looks like we won't need to push your unsound mind like we planned. Harry Baranski is who you are, and it will be better for you to keep it clear in your head."

"Where is Josephine? Are they keeping her from coming to see me?"

The lawyer opened and shut his mouth a few times whilst stuffing his papers back in the briefcase. Finally, words leaked out. "She wears no penitential clothing."

"I wish you would talk plain, Mr. Thigpen."

He looked up from his briefcase with sad eyes and said, "Though she called our office to send someone down to represent you, your wife has not shown the kind of support and participation we'd like to see in a loving spouse. I was told she invited the police to search your garage without a warrant, um, and made it very easy, too easy, for them to find the tools that disabled your father's car. Tell me, Harry, if I may ask a very personal question, is your marriage a good one?"

"Yes, for one night."

Then I told Lawyer Thigpen the whole Josephine Baranski story, starting with Taylor Binns's chickens. He opened and shut his mouth a few times again, shook his head, wacked his knee, clucked his tongue and wiped his eyes. When I finished, he said, "If it is all true, Harry, it is a grim fairy tale."

Next day, Detective Peter O'Malley came down and said I had visitors. "They're people from Appleton and Murren, Harry, four of them, too many for a one-on-one. We can give you a half hour in the interrogation room. Of course, there'll be a guard."

I said, "Appleton and Murren? Let them talk to Josephine-- Josephine is the boss."

"Your wife is too busy right now. You'll have to see them yourself or they'll be sent away."

I could see the detective had his personality mussed by something and was short on his leash. I did not want to upset him with a question, but how did he know Josephine was busy right now? I said, "There's a man named Jonnybo works for her. If you can find him, let them talk to him."

Now Peter O'Malley laughed in the sleepy way that is his real style, "Jeanibeaux? Jean Jeanibeaux?" He said it like Zhon Zhonnybo, dragging out the front parts. "I'm afraid he's busy right now too. It looks like they both will be busy for awhile. Look Harry, these people who are here for you, you want to see them yourself, or what?"

I thought, It is a nice break in a jailbird's day, so I said Sure, lead me to it.

The room was midsize, walls the color of green grapes with a picture on one of a trotting horse pulling a man in their little two wheel cart. The horse was stiff and looked like he had wooden legs, and the driver sat with a ramrod spine. I would not buy a picture like that even though it is popular taste. A long formica table sat in the middle of the room with three steel folding chairs up each side and a water cooler with a big blue jug at the far end.

A guard stood by the water cooler and Detective O'Malley let in three people, two young women and one older. "I'll leave you to your business, Mr. Baranski," he said. "We'll be needing the room in a half hour or so," and smiled friendly and shut the door behind him.

The two young women started talking at the same time, then stopped and started again till they decided who must be first.

"We're all so upset about your trouble, Mr. Baranski," said one dressed in a summer cotton dress with a belt and polka dots. "Everybody says it's a mistake and a shame and pray for your earliest possible release. Isn't that the truth, Miss Aurus?"

"Yes," the second one agreed, taller and blonde, in a business suit, "we want our decision maker back." She lifted an eyebrow with half a smile, and I think winked straight at me.

"Don't we, Miss Steggerly?"

Miss Steggerly said, "The warehouses and office building are leaking from the last storm. There is structural damage. Two building inspectors said we will have to vacate if we don't do extensive repairs right away. They must be brought up to code, he said. Bookkeeping and shipping are in good shape, sir, but sales and purchases are not."

I said, "Sales _and_ purchases?"

The blonde said, "Sales _and_ purchases. We all know you don't like a hands-on approach--" her voice made _hands-on_ come out full of sex-- "but if you plan to be more active in the business, sir, we will wait till you come back before we scout new locations. We really must get out of those buildings like Miss Steggerly says-- or else the new manager you hire today can do it, if that is your pleasure, Mr. Baranski." She hung over the word <u>pleasure</u> and brightened her eyes at me. "Also, the garage is yelling like a stuck hog about those tires we ordered, and the bushel cartons--"

"The tires we ordered?" I said.

"They haven't came in," said Miss Steggerly, "and Russell is rotating wheels off trucks in the shop."

Miss Aurus said, "We've been looking at resumes and seeing a few people for interim general manager, sir. Mrs. Deeping here, and a gentleman waiting outside are our screened candidates. We need your sayso, Mr. Baranski, sir." And while she had her back turned to the others, facing me and pointing behind her at the older woman, she winked again, slow and clear this time. "We will leave you to talk to Mrs. Deeping--"

"No, stay," I said.

The blonde was mighty pleased and gave Miss Steggerly a look with her eyes half closed to show her uppity side for scoring with the boss. It is a look only women can give, for men are stupid about eyelids. Mrs. Deeping took it all in and I could see her taking notes in her head.

I said, "Please tell me a little about yourself, Mrs. Deeping."

She had gray hair tied neat in a bun over a starched collar on a print dress. There was a matching belt with fake leather backing made of paper, and the paper was peeling. Her eyes were dark as anthracite and blinked faster when she thought she made a point. She talked for ten minutes straight about entries and balancing and motor pools and how you should lease instead of buy outright and her twenty-five years with Gimbel brothers up in Philadelphia. Two years ago she retired from there and came south to nurse her old mother who died anyway. And now she needed to do something with herself, like put to use all the knowledge and experience that was wasting time without a job to lay it on. Not once did she let on she knew about her lipstick creeping up the puckers in her lips. Her voice was quiet and full of right thoughts, and I was ready to tell Miss Aurus and Miss

112

Steggerly to sign her on when she stood up herself and thanked me and said she'd send in the gentleman waiting outside.

I said, "Thank you, I am glad you came to visit," and was getting ready to tell her a Dusty Broom story when the blonde showed her out and held the door for the next job hunter to come in.

He was big as a boxcar and limped, with an eyepatch on his left eye tied around his head. His suit was old and the wrong kind for gulf coast heat, but all I saw was a handsome face, a little porky under the chin, and I had to hold my hands together to keep them from shaking.

"Miss Steggerly said, "Mr. Baranski, this here is Mr. Darwin Bascom."

It was Tiny from long, long ago.

"Mr. Bascom has excellent credentials," said Miss Aurus.

Father, I am glad now I didn't let on who I was. I could see in his eyes Tiny Bascom drew a blank on me, and with the hard times he was in, needing a job and a room and steady meals, it would of cramped his style to bring up the bad luck I fetched him back then. And this is right where the lie started, Father, with Tiny that day, because I saw a second chance come open for me, to let Harry Baranski clean up some slops I made with my other names. Is this what fate is, Father? Cripples like me screwing up the lives of people and never making good for the damage? You don't get a second chance yourself because you can't unmake pain you are the reason for. It is always somebody else who must come along and clean up your slops. But here the somebody else is me! This idea has lit up my heart: I must stay Harry Baranski.

Tiny Bascom worked his way through business school, he said, then worked his way up from file clerk to office manager on a Granex onion farm in Texas where I remember he was headed all those years ago. That job took him to Arizona in companies that raised melons, sheep and cattle and also dairying. He took some creased papers out of a pocket and spread them out for me to see. They were payroll stubs and old letterheads. "He said, "Please sir, I need this job and my work was not so

113

different than Appleton and Murren, with foodstuffs and buying and shipping."

I said, "You stayed a bachelor?"

"Yes, but I come east after a girl who turned me down." Now he laughed and blushed a little and looked at Miss Aurus and Miss Steggerly who shook their head at this sad story. "It is partly why I am in this mess-- leaving a good job and no safety net once I got here. My girl married somebody else, and I couldn't eat or sleep or raise myself up to go look for work. It lasted six months, and all the jobs I go out for now, they tell me I am overqualified since they want mostly typing and file clerks."

"Overqualified is better than underqualified," I said.

Tiny smiled; he was nervous. "To be honest, I am about broke, though that's no reason to hire me. What I'm saying is, I'll take any opening you have and then show you what I can do. The companies I was with, they all did well. They all made money and got busier and bigger. I know the business; please give me a chance, please."

The ladies dabbed their eye with hankies and coughed to get down their throat lump. I said, "Miss Steggerly and Miss Aurus, I think Mrs. Deeping is a fine lady with plenty experience and won't have any trouble finding herself a job. That makes me feel good about hiring Mr. Bascom for this one. See he gets a little advance to set him back on his feet and bring him in to work right away to learn the ropes and particulars."

"Thank you, thank you sir," he said and shook my hand.

"You already said Please, Mr. Bascom. When you say Please, you don't have to say thank you." I remember this was advice I gave him before, when we were boys on the road.

After he left and I was alone with Miss Aurus and Miss Steggerly, I said, "What's going on? Mr. Jonnybo is the general manager and Josephine Baranski has the sayso. Either one of them do the hiring. And why is Appleton and Murren needing a new general manager when Mr. Jonnybo is already?"

Miss Steggerly fumbled a minute, looking at the blonde for help, who was shifting from one foot to the other. Then she said, "I guess you haven't seen a paper or TV for a couple days, right? Because--"

Miss Aurus jumped in all excited, "They are arrested for questioning. They've been here, right here, since this morning!"

Later I got it from Detective Talley and Lawyer Thigpen that this was true. Also, the lawyer said, "When I was a boy in school, the other children called me Pigpen."

10

Getting Is Not The Same As Taking

"A generous spirit enhances mediocrity as well as genius," said Lawyer Thigpen. "Have you ever thought about that, Harry?"

But I was looking at his suit, a double-breasted pinstripe, pink-tint shirt with cufflinks. Then I looked at the green walls and the horse pulling the man. We were in the same room that I met Tiny Bascom again only this time we waited for Detective O'Malley. "Mediocrity?" I said.

"Being a dummy."

"Is this a riddle?"

"Robert Frost would have been a better poet if he'd been a decent human being, and Beasely McAllister a better judge. I trust you know I mean Robert Frost's genius and Beasely McCallister's mediocrity?"

"I have not had the pleasure of neither one, Mr. Thigpen."

"Robert Frost questioned the road he'd taken in life, and Judge McCallister never questioned anything. If Frost had shared the spirit of generosity of, say, Gandhi or Christ, his question would not even have occurred to him, and if the judge had likewise shared, he would not have been able to stop questioning."

"Dusty Broom told me questions put people on the spot."

"Dusty Broom? Who's Dusty Broom?"

"A man I used to know. He also said not asking questions makes people think you don't care."

Lawyer Thigpen rubbed his chin a minute. "Asking questions and not asking questions end you up at the same place? Mr. Broom can't make up his mind, can he?"

I did not like the tone of his meaning. "Same as you sir, for if Mr. Frost stopped asking his question and Judge McCallister started up with his, then they have only traded places, and the genius and the dummy are the same."

The lawyer laughed, "I see your point, Harry, but Frost will live forever and Beasely McCallister will eat the same dirt as the killers and drug dealers he sets loose. Nobody remembers their names either."

I was beginning to think of Ralph again and what he would make of the trouble I'm in when Peter O'Malley stuck his head through the door and said hello in molasses speed. "Sorry to cut y'all off, boys, but I'm sending a guard in here. The prisoners will be brought up as soon as their lawyers come. It'll only be a few more minutes." Then he opened the door wider and a guard slack-walked over to the water cooler. Detective O'Malley ducked out.

Prisoners, he said.

"They're to be arraigned today," said Lawyer Thigpen.

"You must be reading my mind. What happened? How'd they catch on to Josephine? And Jonnybo? I never thought of him at all."

Lawyer Thigpen shot his cuffs and said, "Can't say; part of the deal. You'll see for yourself in a few minutes. They want you uncoached, and I gave my word. Marshall Thigpen's word is Wells Fargo secure, everybody knows that. But I can say you are out of danger unless they dig up a surprise or two for us. Later on today, your wife and Jeanibeaux will enter a plea and bail will be set. If all goes well, charges against you will be dismissed and you can get back to your business and your life."

I chilled up my back, "You told me once your job was to save me from the rope. Are they still going to stretch my neck?"

"Not quite, I think, but I can't take the credit," said Lawyer Thigpen with a headshake. "It's human frailty, Harry; arrogance, mostly. You'll see. I am sorry about your wife, however."

"Will they give me back my own clothes?"

"What? Oh, yes. Yes, of course they--"

The door opened and Detective O'Malley backed in talking to two men, white, and a lady, black-- all in good suits who were following and yapping at him together. Then came Josephine and Jonnybo, looking mussed, and two guards behind. They took seats around the table, all but one of the men in a suit, tall, young, bald with rimless glasses, and Peter O'Malley. The detective came around and sat next to me while the tall man stood behind me and Lawyer Thigpen. The two other suits turned out to be separate lawyers for Josephine and Jonnybo.

One of them, next to Jonnybo, an older squatty man with popeyes and wiry hair slicked together by vaseline, said, "You haven't told us how you can make a charge with no positive I.D. on the body. If there's no Greg Loomis, how can you say Greg Loomis is the body? We've combed the national wires and the federal computer files-- there's no record that Greg Loomis ever existed, anywhere."

"Right on," said the black lady lawyer who sat next to Josephine.

"Please, Counselor, don't waste our time," said the young man standing behind us. "My mother isn't in the files, and neither are a few million other good people who don't vote, don't work for government and stay out of trouble. You will acknowledge that we have a body, won't you, folks? My office says that's enough. You already know it has Greg Loomis's bank passbook, his library card and a few charge cards. Let's drop the red herrings and just say it's Greg Loomis so we can move forward with this meeting-- we're doing it as a courtesy, you know. It's a chance to save your clients the humiliation of a trial and maybe save their skin-- and it will look good on your resume. Otherwise beware, we've got stuff any jury will love."

This young man was an assistant county prosecutor whose eyes had bags beneath his glasses; lawyering must be hard work if you do it right. Also, his hands had cracked calluses with dirt grained tight in them. I could see he must do hand labor on weekends to boost up the pay of a county grunt. His name was Arthur Galindez.

The black lady lawyer whose name was Ras-Al Jenkins, said, "What about your resume, Mr. Galindez? Why would you squash a trial where you could look like a hero, if you've got the killer evidence you say you've got?"

"Peter," the assistant prosecutor waved at his detective who bobbed his head and opened a notebook.

"In the pocket of the jacket Greg Loomis was wearing we found the following: one belt, or sash, known to be worn as a hair ribbon, or decoration, by Mrs. Josephine Baranski and identified as hers by three members of the office staff at Appleton and Murren. One pair of silver earrings inlaid with semiprecious stones, also identified by office staff. A handwritten note, still legible, of intimate content, signed Josephine. This note is presently under analysis by an expert forensic graphologist. There was also a bank passbook showing a $200 deposit, recently made, as well as several credit cards affirming Greg Loomis's identity. He was an employee of Appleton and Murren."

"Is that it?" said the squatty lawyer, named Ockenlander. He went on with a mean streak in his tone that had an edge of laughing on it, like people who think they have got you boxed and can't stand waiting to let the lions loose on you or they will piss theirself. "Mr. Galindez, if Greg Loomis stole Josephine Baranski's car, could he not also have stolen her personal belongings?"

Instead of answering, the assistant prosecutor took off his specs and huffed on them with a eat-your-canary grin. As he wiped them on a hanky, he bobbed his head at Detective O'Malley again.

"We have an eyewitness who picked Josephine Baranski and Jean Jeanibeaux out of separate line-ups yesterday. He subsequently pulled their mug shots out of a random sample of fifty others. He will testify that Mr. Jeanibeaux checked into the Citrus Queen motel-- we have the sign-in card-- a day before Josephine Baranski's car was reported stolen, and that he gave Mr. Jeanibeaux an envelope as instructed by Mrs. Baranski when she paid for the room. We have reason to believe that the envelope contained the note signed Josephine and the two hundred dollars credited in the bank passbook in Greg Loomis's pocket. We believe the note was passed to Mr. Loomis and that he put it in his pocket without the knowledge of Mrs. Baranski and Mr. Jeanibeaux. The witness will further testify that at five thirty PM that same evening, Mrs. Baranski picked up Mr.

Jeanibeaux in her car, the red BMW reported stolen less than twelve hours later."

Jonnybo was fire-eyed and spitting curses in Lawyer Ockenlander's ear. He waved his hands and pounded one fist in a palm with loud smacking noises, whispering and moaning and breathing hard. Like all bullies, he was folding.

"Who is your eyewitness?" said Ras-Al Jenkins, "some cataracted senior just this side of Alzheimer's?"

Assistant Prosecutor Galindez said, "We'll let you know in plenty of time if you decide to go on with this. But I can tell you, he is a young man with perfect eyesight and a steeltrap memory."

No, I thought, he is a stoned, dyehaired, pothead knee-wacking rocksucker who, in a mystery, mistook Jonnybo for me. He is the pink roomclerk who I signed Jonnybo's name with.

"That's not all," said Arthur Galindez, "as soon as we get the details worked out, we will be charging your clients with the murder of Peter Paul Baranski also, since it is Jean Jeanibeaux's prints all over the tools Josephine Baranski led our office to, and none of Harry Baranski's. We expect our garage to provide other incriminating evidence. Already we have fibers that match a coat belonging to Mr. Jeanibeaux, found in Mrs. Baranski's bedroom closet. Your name is sewn inside, Mr. Jeanibeaux-- how careless can you get? Control of Appleton and Murren was your motive, a very lucrative business. You were lovers, conspirators and killers, and though we don't know why you murdered Greg Loomis, sooner or later we'll get that too." Then he came around to where we could see him and said, "Mr. Thigpen, your client is free to go." And to me, "Mr. Baranski, you have our most sincere apology."

Ras-Al Jenkins said to Josephine, "Don't worry, Honey. You'll be back home by tomorrow. They'll set bail at the arraignment."

"I'll drop you off at your place, Harry," Marshall Thigpen said.

For two days I played with my new house, pushing buttons and watching walls slide and machines start to operate someplace in another room or a robot voice giving me directions or asking questions. I made my own meals out of a refrigerator full of food and two freezers packed with enough to take care of the rush hour crowd at the Locutan diner for a month. I tried on all of Harry Baranski's clothes-- my clothes-- which fit; we are a perfect size 40 off the rack, though his are made to order, and put on one of our tennis outfits and went out to the tennis court where I tested it, bouncing up & down in our tennis shoes. Inside a bedroom dresser drawer, I found $2462 in tens, fives and ones with a rubber band around it. Next to the money was Harry Baranski's wallet with all his cards, registrations and a few family pictures. After lunch, I laid on a lounge by the pool listening to music from a button I found on the outdoor bar made to look like a Hawaiian hut and jumped in for a swim when the sun baked too hard. In the garage were three cars: a Land Rover, a little two-seat Mercedes, and a big Jaguar sedan, and stuck on hooks on a wall were the keys.

There was a feeling somebody would come along and throw me out of there, for belonging takes time and must be got used to, so I jammed in as much rich living as I could, thinking once in awhile if only Ralph could be here to taste of it, so different this was from what life set us up for. It sometimes makes your stomach ache to think what dead folks are missing. But there was a housecleaner and a pool boy and four men to cut & trim the grounds, all saying Mr. Baranski this and Mr. Baranski that, till I started to get the hang of it and answered to the name right away. Then just before dinnertime on the second day, a delivery came for Harry Baranski-- a box of Punch imported cigars-- which I signed for in my new name. The rest of the night, I smoked a cigar and stopped feeling I did not belong there and slept in the middle of the big bed without worrying that I must lay only on the edge to jump up and run off if discovered.

"I told her I'd call you for her, Harry," said Detective Peter O'Malley next morning on the telephone. "Bail was denied on both of them just an hour ago. I think she's getting the idea what kind of trouble she's in. She's asking for you. It's okay, she's allowed visitors. Use the side entrance; it goes right upstairs to the waiting room."

I told him I would come, then got dressed with Harry Baranski's wallet in my pocket and drove the little Mercedes over to the county jail. The side entrance was not busy, a few people in & out and up & down a steep stairway. The walls were peeling paint and the place smelt like a wet, punky cellar. At the first landing, the newel post was rotted out, only held up by the balusters and top rail.

Up in the waiting room, Peter O'Malley was already there. I counted six others sitting around reading and talking. "You look nice, Harry," he said, "though you are a little peaked, like you have dropped a few pounds. This has been a nightmare experience for you, son. I only hope you have learned a lesson, that it has made you strong. I only hope you will profit by it."

This was a nice thought, but one I could not answer to, for profit has a front door & a back door and the detective must never know which one I took in. I have made a profit on work I never did. I have made a profit on the bad luck of other people. I said, "You've got a rotted out newel post on the first landing of that staircase out there. The stairs are too steep and somebody in a hurry will kill theirself. I can fix it for you if you get me some tools. I am handy with tools."

Detective O'Malley laughed and said, "Tools are not in the budget, Harry. Things are fixed around here only after they break. Look, there's something I have to tell you before you go in to see your wife-- it's about Jeanibeaux."

"Jonnybo," I said, like it was a haunt.

"There was a paperwork technicality, a back office screwup. He was arrested on a wrong warrant-- we had to release him. His lawyer was screaming bloody hell--"

"Release him? He-- he'll come--"

The detective said, "He won't come anywhere. They're working up a new warrant, and as soon as we get it signed, he'll be rearrested."

"You expect him to wait around for that?"

"He's still in the building-- don't worry yourself about him, Harry. Go on in and talk to your wife now, go on."

So I went through a couple doors where guards passed me by a machine and waved wands around me and finally let me into a

123

room with a long double row of chairs facing each other, each chair at the end of a small table and a framed wire mesh screen screwed into the middle of the table between the chairs. Two people were up at the far end talking low through the screen to prisoners. Josephine was sitting near the door and smiled when I took a chair. She was wearing an orange suit.

"Hello Greggy," she said. "We messed up big time, huh?"

I said, "I am Harry Baranski, and I didn't mess up at all. Who is Greggy?"

"I didn't mean you, I meant us-- we messed up, Jean and me. Or, to be right about it, you messed us up. You left my things in the jacket Jean put on Harry."

I looked around to make sure of no spies. "I am Harry. You wanted to stick me with Peter Paul's murder."

"Keep your voice down, will you?"

I whispered, "The prosecutor already knows, and it will all come out at your trial anyhow-- if you are dumb enough to go for a trial."

Josephine squawked like a cat, "Don't be stupid, that's why you're still out there free. Haven't you wondered why we didn't expose you?"

"And dig yourself a deeper hole?" I said. "Not only did you kill your husband's father and your husband also, but you tried to frame the stranger whose name you gave your husband's body. I am Harry Baranski, all south Florida knows that. My fingerprints are in Washington by now--"

"You are out there because one of us has to be out there," said Josephine. "One of us has to be free to help the others."

"You are nuts."

"I thought you loved me, Greggy. Did you forget our times together? You were hot. I made you hot."

She did, it is true, but I knew if I wanted to be hot again, it must be with somebody else. I ignored her point and asked one of my own. "One thing," I said, "how did that pothead room clerk pick Jonnybo out of a line-up?"

Josephine caught on I was not the same jerk I was a few days ago. She cooled off and came back again, this time softer, sly. "Jean came into the office with me when I paid for your room.

The pothead must've fixed on him-- I don't know. And then you sign in with his name. Is-- is it just coincidence, or maybe--"

"What?"

"Maybe a grand plan?"

"I go for number two."

"We'll make it worth your while, Greg. Tell them the thief stole your jacket-- Greg Loomis stole your jacket; you're Harry, remember-- stole your jacket with my things in it before he stole the car. A wife gives her husband things to hold, doesn't she-- ribbons and earrings and such? The passbook and other cards were separate, in the new wallet in his back pocket. Jean made sure to put it there, in his back pocket. My things were in the jacket, your jacket, Harry, and had a right to be there. It was a perfect plan and it can be perfect again. Tell them it is your jacket and the thief stole it. We'll make you richer than you ever dreamed."

I said, "Too late, I'm already rich. I am Harry Baranski. If I knew you were a killer, I never would of loved you. Take my advice and confess, but don't tell them the truth or they will put you in the loony bin. Just confess you killed Peter Paul Baranski and Greg Loomis, and blame Jonnybo-- you will get off easier. I am sure he put you up to it."

"Oh yes," she said with her eyes round and full of tears, "he did. He did!"

"You are beautiful," I said, getting out of my chair with a big sigh. "Dusty Broom once told me it is a shame that beauty always hits a higher note than trust and grace and duty done." "Who is Dusty Broom?"

I shook my head a little and said, "You don't remember-- I am not surprised."

*

Back in the waiting room I sat down and closed my eyes in a soft chair. Josephine is a woman who fills up your heart, and all the people she pushed out would find it hard to push back in, so I thought of them coughing up dust at the bottom of my memory and saw the spark of a face I remembered or heard a voice I knew from long ago. In the waiting room, people passed by, sat down, got up, said a few words here & there.

"You going to do what she asked?"

It was Jonnybo's voice and I sat straight up. He was on a sofa next to my chair with conversation on his face so's not to let on to the public who he was or what he was up to. I saw his lawyer, Mr. Ockenlander, across the room pretending not to listen. "You mean lie about the jacket?" I said.

"No lie if you say it's Harry Baranski's jacket on that body; how else would Greg Loomis be wearing it unless he stole it?"

"No, it is Greg Loomis's jacket all right."

"Name your price."

"No."

"We'll bring you down with us."

I said, "If it's no lie, why don't you get your lawyer to bring it up? I'll tell you why-- it's the note together with the other things also in that jacket. She tempted Greg Loomis and then you both killed him, but he put all that stuff in his pocket, and you never even checked it out. You are as dumb as a horse."

Jonnybo leaned closer to me and dribbled out his hate in a whisper. "I'll track you down; I'll trail you to the end of the earth. First I'll kill everything you love, and then I'll kill you. You put us in this mess, you ratfaced little bastard, and even if it takes forever, you will never be safe."

"If that's your dream, you will be dreaming it in jail," I said.

He stood up but leaned down to me in my chair. "They'll never get me to a jail." Now I saw Lawyer Ockenlander standing by the stairwell door, holding it open. The waiting room was empty-- they had waited till it was empty.

"Hurry," said Mr. Ockenlander with a tight voice.

Jonnybo rushed out the door and I could hear his feet clacking down the stairs fainter & fainter until a creaking sound and a loud squerk, then crashing and rattling and yells of pain.

The police ambulance took him to a hospital where he had a broken ankle and a foot, for the newel post on the downstairs landing gave way when he grabbed it and swung around full weight on the run. I told Detective O'Malley the story and he said they would add <u>escaping</u> to Jonnybo's charges and also look into Lawyer Ockenlander's part.

When we were alone, late, in the empty waiting room, he shook my hand and held onto it. "In the beginning, you insisted you were not Harry Baranski. I'll tell you now, I didn't believe it, of course, but I wondered what you were up to. Now I do believe it, I do believe you're not Harry Baranski, but it isn't something I'd want to prove even if I could. And d'you know why, son? It's because, whoever you are, you're a better Harry Baranski than the other one, the last one. You've got heart, and courage. I do think you've got courage, and I'll be watching you for it, son, not to keep track of or tabs on, but only to see how good a Baranski can be." Then he let loose my hand and didn't look back on the way to the stairwell door.

Next day, I called the Goodwill people to send a truck to the house and spent the rest of the day emptying out all of Josephine's clothes and doodads. Two days later, the six o'clock news said Josephine Baranski confessed her part in the murders of Peter Paul Baranski and Greg Loomis, but said she was not in her right mind from love, which put her under a spell following Jonnybo's orders. The newslady asked a TV lawyer what motive there was to kill Greg Loomis, a stranger, and the lawyer said if there is a confession you don't need a motive. Then a panel of experts decided it must of been a sex triangle with Greg Loomis, an employee, finally in the way.

Dusty Broom told me that people have only two sides-- inside & outside. But there is also good side and bad side, upside and downside, soft side and hard side. Jonnybo only showed me one side, yet he must love his mother, his dog. Josephine showed me two sides and also showed that there was another side she kept hid, and by doing that, showed it too in the end. People can show only one side at a time, for if they could show them all at once, it would be the end of the world.

You know the rest, Father; and the confession I made to you, I now cancel the rules of. Tell my friends for me. It is time to go.

*

127

Appendix

I am Charles Allensworth, Bishop of Locutan, Florida. The preceding memoir was delivered to me by messenger several months ago, and, enjoined by conscience, my staff and I spent weeks in deliberation regarding its disposition. Since Frank Farley-- for so we knew him here-- stipulates in his final lines the release from confidentiality of his sacramental confession to this office, I have, with some misgiving, deduced his permission to publish these notes as well. The final reasoning was: if the confession was meant to be executory, so too is the memoir.

We believe that Frank Farley's story deserves the widest possible audience, for it is a story, above all, of perseverence. That this quality should have yielded the striking advantages to Locutan's economic, social, cultural, educational and recreational welfare as it has done, could not have been predicted or foreseen by anyone who knew him. He was hard-working and dogged; he was humorous and kind; he was inquisitive and helpful; he was single-minded and honest; he was careful and nurturing, but to what degree, no one suspected. It is clear to us now that many unseen elements of character lie dormant in the human heart which come to light only if opportunity frees them. No one knew it then, but as he makes plain here to all the world, Frank Farley's opportunity came suddenly and hugely upon him and was turned immediately to the care of others.

He sometimes observed the calamitous effect his presence seemed to generate upon events and people close to him. It is true enough, machines broke down and mysterious ailments filled the air when he was around, accidents happened regularly. But were these the outcome of coincidence-- the consequent happening at the end of many antecedent happenings? Or, as he had come to believe, were they some dark, abusive emanation of his personality? No one who knew him in Locutan thought else but the best of him.

Upon resolution of his entanglements with the justice system and incarceration of both felons responsible for his own difficulties, he purchased two warehouse properties in Locutan and transferred to them the entire inventory, motor pool and administrative offices of Appleton and Murren Import/Export out of their unsuitable facilities in Fort Myers. He did this without the sacrifice of a single position, and, in fact, increased staff by 10% through this move. With the knowledgeable intervention of his comptroller, Mr. Darwin Bascom, he engaged the services of Dexter Philpot Construction to build additional warehouse, garage and office space as needed, later assisting Mr. Philpot in the incorporation of his growing business, now called Philpot Modular, Inc. He also instructed Mr. Bascom to oversee conversion of Esau Philpot's chicken farm to productive citrus groveland, now called Philpot Groves, Inc.

At this point, perhaps anticipating questions of legal ownership down the line, he took Appleton and Murren public, helping in the selection of its Board of Directors in order to stymie the possibility of a challenge if and when his true identity should become known. The company now belongs to its stockholders and is the heart and pulse of this growing little city. (He has placed his own shares in a trust to be administered by the Harry Baranski Foundation, the philanthropic arm of his Appleton and Murren legacy to Locutan. The trust, however, is revocable, for Frank Farley, though sometimes naive regarding worldly matters, is not a fool.)

He never came to Locutan, but conducted such business as required his attention from a home office in Punta Rasa, communicating with local facilities by telephone and computer. It was at Punta Rasa that he formulated his philanthropies and city-based ventures: construction by Philpot Modular of a new city library; rebuilding by Philpot Modular of the old lightning-struck Baptist church-- now the Combined Church of Locutan, which includes the RC Church's diocesan headquarters; establishment of the Baranski Trust bank with loans to the working poor at interest rates lower than any similar institution in the state of Florida; construction by Philpot Modular of Locutan's first shopping mall with multiplex theater; architectural and site planning of a cultural arts center with 50% financing in place, matching funds to be provided by state and county taxing authorities, and founding of the Esau Philpot

Research Laboratory at Philpot Groves for the development of frost-proof citrus crops.

Mr. Peter O'Malley, retired detective of the Fort Myers PD, supervised the creation of, and continues to head a 68 member security force for all of the Baranski holdings. In addition, a private venture, O'Malleysafe, Inc., provides domestic and commercial monitoring services up and down the west coast of Florida. Now residing in Locutan, Mr. O'Malley has proven to be an acute and forceful local leader in civic matters.

Grandy Cumberhouse recovered completely and robustly from the pneumonia that burdened her during Frank Farley's last days here. She and Taylor Binns were married in the Combined Church of Locutan, the present writer presiding, and with the guidance of Darwin Bascom, began what is now Binns Transportation Systems, Inc., the largest and most reliable local train, bus, shuttle and taxi service in south Florida. It has been rumored that Mr. Binns plans to inaugurate a shuttle flight route to Miami International Airport in the near future.

Valerio, the dog, has fathered several litters and continues to show distaste for Taylor Binns.

I have been able to give up my supplemental employment-- the gag writing and short-order cooking.

All of this has been accomplished in the past six and one half years.

*

But I have saved the best surprise for last.

Shortly after he assumed personal responsibility for the operation of Appleton and Murren, "Harry Baranski" sent word of a job offer for Household Manager to Elsie Allensworth, my daughter. The position comprised hiring staff for interior and exterior maintenance, including swimming pool, tennis courts and landscaping; and responsibility for household cuisine, decor and victual inventories, with dog kennel and stable understood to be a part of the household. The salary was ample, and all meals and a private apartment on the grounds would be provided.

Elsie accepted the offer, and after a week's orientation, took over the job. She excelled at this work, displaying a growing knowledge of business matters and their administration. Her visits home were filled with accounts of Frank Farley's understanding and generosity as well as her own growth and achievement. Her happiness was my fulfillment. During the sixth year of her residence at Punta Rasa, she and Frank Farley were married as Mr. & Mrs. Harry Baranski. Six months later, after designating powers of attorney to Darwin Bascom and certain other members of the board, they sold the estate at Punta Rasa and began the travels that have taken them far from home. It was at this point that the Farley memoir was sent to me.

I hear from Elsie every few months, and even got a card from Frank last year. There are no children yet, but I am hopeful. They seem to be inching their way to the northwest. Although what I first saw as his self-loathing seems to have come under Frank's control, it is possible he still feels he needs redeeming. Maybe he is going there to look for his brother's grave and for whatever else he and Ralph left behind-- to put his selves together at last.

I have sometimes wondered why he left when he did. Perhaps because his local expiation took exactly six and a half years? He once said <u>When you're even, throw in your cards and leave the game</u>.

Dusty Broom told him that.

With this seal,
Msgr C. Allensworth
Bishop of Locutan

Fortiter in re

<u>Member of the Board</u>:
Appleton and Murren, Inc.
Baranski Trust Bank
Philpot Modular, Inc.
Philpot Groves, Inc.
Binns Trans Systems, Inc.

About the Author

Monk Rose has been a boxer, shopkeeper, school teacher, freelance writer and professional musician. He has written for journals and magazines, and his fiction and poetry have previously been published. He lives in Florida with his wife where he is presently at work on his eighteenth book.